"What a beautiful book: a simple but radical point of point of view, a generative interpretation of goodness and being change, as well as a practical way to embark on this journey."

—**Richard Strozzi-Heckler, PhD**, author of The *Leadership Dojo* and *In Search of the Warrior Spirit*

"A fascinating exploration of how we are all interconnected as living beings on this wondrous planet, *Resonate* weaves the often disparate fields of physics and contemplative practice into an immersion in how we can bring more well-being into our personal and collective lives. Ginny Whitelaw ably guides us through accessible math and meditation, science and subjective experience, to feel the reality of our interdependent lives and how we might work together to bring positive change into our world."

—**Daniel J. Siegel, MD**, *New York Times* bestselling author of *Aware: The Science and Practice of Presence* and *The Developing Mind*

"The evolution from ego to Essence is the transcendent, transformative journey of life. *Resonate* gives you exceptionally clear and compelling practices to navigate this 'Zen On-Purpose' passage. Ginny Whitelaw is a master, a leader for life, someone who truly 'Leads the Way.' Get this book as your trail guide for purpose-driven awakening."

—**Kevin Cashman**, Global Leader CEO & Executive Development, Korn Ferry, and bestselling author of *Leadership from the Inside Out* and *The Pause Principle*

"Whitelaw Roshi is a scientist at heart. She likes her Zen to be palpable and practical. So when she talks resonance, she doesn't open her mouth unless she is already resonating with all that surrounds her. You either feel it, and the lesson sinks in. Or you don't feel it, and go back to the *Zazen* cushion until you do."

–**Gordon Greene Roshi**, Spring Green Dojo

"In her latest groundbreaking book, Dr. Ginny Whitelaw explains the science of energy in terms we can all understand, and then shows us how to use resonance to improve the energy of our marriages, our workplaces, and even—if you're fearless—the world. Dear Change Agents, this is your book."

—**Rebecca Ryan**, CEO, Futurist and Economist,
author of *ReGENERATION*

"This brilliant book offers you a view of the world through the lens of interconnection. Dr. Ginny Whitelaw takes you through a multi-dimensional journey using the principles of resonance to unpack the scientific, emotional, organizational and global implications of what is possible when we learn to resonate with the world around us. From the sublime to the practical, her book invites you to discover ways to become a 'Universal Energy Concentrator that . . . turns ideas into things that matter . . .'"

—**Wendy Palmer**, founder of Leadership Embodiment, author of
The Intuitive Body and The Practice of Freedom

"Stop spinning your wheels trying to get buy-in! *Resonate* offers fresh teachings to learn how to refine your body-mind instrument to work in flow with others and skillfully sync ideas that matter with those you seek to influence."

—**Cara Bradley**, body-mind performance coach and author of
On The Verge: Wake up, Show up and Shine

"This book is of fundamental importance! These times call us beyond the superficial and habitual layers of our experience. Now is the time to refine ourselves as an instrument, fine-tuned to the principle at the heart of all change: resonance. This excellent book shows you how."

–**Joel Monk**, co-founder of Coaches Rising

"In *Resonate*, Ginny Whitelaw's words ring out with clarity, wisdom, and depth. It's an easy and lively read that steers clear of unnecessary technicalities while staying true to the heart of physics and philosophy. Above all, this is a book of practical wisdom that teaches you how to listen acutely for the resonance that naturally amplifies your gifts and your contribution."

–**Amanda Blake**, author of *Your Body is Your Brain*

"Ginny's head, heart and *hara* show up in this remarkable book that guides readers in the process of pragmatically attuning their own resonance with others and with the world. Reading *Resonate* gives me hope that we can be the instrument of change to address the deep personal and global issues we face today."

—**Chris Johnson, PsyD**. Founder of Q4 Consulting, Inc. and the Core Presence Institute

"'Become the other and go from there.' This is at the heart of the ability to resonate with something larger—your partner, your team, your organization, or perhaps your purpose in life—to change the world. Ginny Whitelaw has lived her life helping people translate themselves into energy for others. This book reveals her journey, her philosophy and her practices. You will not be the same once you read it."

—**Stephen Rhinesmith**, author of *A Manager's Guide to Globalization*

"This book would be remarkable simply for the way it makes the insights of physics and Zen accessible to the lay reader. Yet what is astonishing is how deftly Ginny Whitelaw shows us how to turn those insights into action. With pragmatism and clarity informed by decades of experience, she shows how each of us can harness the power of resonance to change ourselves, our companies, our world. Step into Resonance. As she says, the times demand it."

—**Ed Bernard**, Retired Vice Chairman T. Rowe Price

Resonate: Zen and the Way of
Making a Difference

by Ginny Whitelaw

ISBN 978-1-64663-136-0

Published by

köehlerbooks™

3705 Shore Drive
Virginia Beach, VA 23455
800-435-4811
www.koehlerbooks.com

RESONATE

Zen and the Way of Making a Difference

Ginny Whitelaw

VIRGINIA BEACH
CAPE CHARLES

To the divine nature in you
and the difference it can make

TABLE OF CONTENTS

INTRODUCTION

The world is a noisy place where it can be hard to be heard. The times are disruptive, where blindsiding forces hit families, businesses, organizations, and societies, and it can be hard to adapt. The institutions of our world, from polarized governments to lumbering healthcare systems, show deepening cracks of dysfunction, where they're not up to the challenges we face. And the heating up of our planet puts a ticking time bomb on all of this, making it hard to pretend we can just keep doing what we've been doing and everything will be OK. And here we are—you and I—with a pair of hands and feet, a love for some part of this world—maybe even all of it—and a set of gifts, a sense of purpose coming through us. How do we make a difference in this vast sea of confusion? How do we gain traction on seemingly intractable problems? How do we live a life of meaning, buoyed by resilience, and imbued with joy? There is a Way, and the purpose of this book is to show it and share it.

Beneath the many waves of the confused sea that is our present reality, there is one principle underlying all change. It's a principle we also participate in, can get a sense for, and even master. That principle is resonance and this book is your guide.

This book itself grew out of resonance. I was teaching a program last year at the Institute for Zen Leadership in which Gordon Greene Roshi gave a passionate talk about climate change. He probed why it's so darn difficult for people to change their habits, indeed, which it's so hard for him to change his own habits. His son, Sam, a world-class scientist and Rhodes Scholar, has been a voice for shrinking our footprint on the planet ever since he was a young boy. Habits in the Greene household attest to his influence, from the energy-efficient heating system to the absence of aluminum foil. Sam manages his carbon footprint like others manage their stock portfolios. And he inspired Gordon to calculate his own carbon footprint, which Gordon spoke to us about that night. "How do we get to a tipping point on this issue?" Gordon asked. "How do we change how change happens?"

Gordon's talk resonated with Glynnis Rengger, the CEO of The Immersion Lab. Her company takes leaders into markets and other organizations to more deeply understand what's going on, where the needs are, and how they need to respond. Something about Zen and Zen leadership training and what it could do for a big, hairy issue like changing our habits around climate change started niggling on her. "I have to do something with this," she said by the end of the program. And this is not a woman who needed something else to do. But she did something. She proceeded to convene a series of workshops bringing together multiple generations, Zen practitioners, leaders, and scientists—including Sam—to explore how Zen could change our glacial approach to climate change before the glaciers all disappear.

Gordon's talk and Glynnis' commitment further resonated with me: "How do we change how change happens?" Instantly, answers started vibrating through me, as if they were running up the two prongs of a tuning fork, reinforcing one another with every bounce. The physicist in me said, *Change always happens the same way: through resonance. We have to change the conditions for resonance to occur.* The Zen teacher in me said, *Our training is all about resonance and how human beings can be one-with the energies of nature, of life, of the universe.* The physicist said, *Show the principles of resonance, and people will see what's present or missing in the change they want to make.* The Zen teacher said, *Help people embody the principles, and develop their sensitivity to naturally vibrate with the change that is theirs to make.* The physicist said, *Show people how to scale up change.* And the Zen teacher knew, *We have something to offer that could be game-changing at a time when our game surely needs to change.*

The idea for *Resonate* wouldn't let me go. I fought it for a few weeks because, like Glynnis, I didn't need more to do. But every time I meditated, new parts of it popped up. Life kept presenting opportunities to explore it further, as when I was teaching a group of Zen priests-in-training about the role of chanting (*okyo*) in our tradition. It's not about ritual, but resonance, and using the vibration of sound to change the resonance of the human body, like tuning a musical instrument. The energy for this book kept building, changing me, changing my priorities. Two week-long trips within in a month suddenly got cancelled and—there it was—a freed-up calendar. I had enough time to immerse myself in writing to see if this book really wanted to happen. In fits and starts, it kept building steam. Like a hologram slowly coming into focus, and then snapping to clarity, it came into being. About a week later, out of the "nowhere" that is the energy connecting us all, came an email from Tre Wee, at Publishizer—a crowd-sourcing platform for authors and their books. Did I have a project that I might want to pitch on their platform? Did I indeed!

Six months later, also out of the "nowhere" connecting all us, came a virus that upended our world, forcing us to resonate with radically new conditions—ready or not—and making practices for resonating effectively more relevant than ever. From realizing goals to adjusting to tragedy, resonance plays in all of it. So, how can resonance play in your life? Is it as simple as wishing our dreams to reality? Or "build it and they will come"? Yes and no. The "yes" part is that if what we wish for matches what's ready to happen, then adding our energy to it *can* bring it into reality. If people have a need or hunger for what we want to build, yes, if we build it, they will come. But the "no" part is that if a thought in our mind is just peculiar to us, or if our head and heart don't agree and we're not integrated in realizing our dream, we send mixed signals and don't manifest our dream. The truth is, our normal state as human beings is one of some dis-harmony and dis-integration: gaps in our awareness, conflict in our life, awkwardness in our actions, trauma from our childhood or our parents' parents' childhood, all create sticking points for us in the present.

As a metaphor, imagine you're opening a large cardboard box. Maybe you've seen the vintage cartoon series where Road Runner is always chased by and then outwitting Wile E. Coyote, who in turn is forever ordering exotic contraptions that arrive in a large box. If so, you can see ACME written on the side of this box because, just like something Coyote would order, it contains a magnificent instrument: a Universal Energy Concentrator. As advertised, it can turn dreams into reality, ideas into actions, YES, it can actually turn energy into things that matter. You can't wait to try it out, but you can't figure out how to get it working. You throw a few dreams into it, but nothing happens. And, oh dear, there's a few broken parts rolling around in the bottom of the box, it's out of tune, and the darn thing seems to have a mind of its own. Worse yet, it didn't come with any instructions.

How do you get this thing working? How can you use it to materialize your goals and realize your dreams? These are urgent matters because the contraption in question is none other than your own mind-body. At its best, it can resonate with the energy of the universe, concentrate it through your skills, gifts, and intentions, and direct it into the playing field of everyday human affairs.

And now I'm not speaking metaphorically—OK, the cardboard ACME box was a metaphor—but here's the truth of your existence: you are part energy and part matter. And life, from birth to death, is a flow of energy that keeps materializing. Resonance is the unifying principle by which energy changes to matter, matter changes form, and all change comes about. Moreover, it's a principle you can leverage to realize dreams, make a difference, and live your most significant life. This book will help you master resonance, not as a theoretical idea, but as a direct experience by which you can use your mind-body-as-one to work with the energy around you and co-create with it. It answers three questions:

- How is it that resonance does everything?
- How can you become a more resonant being?
- How can you use resonance to make a difference?

Far from crystals and magic, this work is grounded in physics, neuroscience, Zen, and leadership, or at least that's how it arose in me and how I'll bring it you. Part I tackles the first question, exploring how resonance materializes change on every scale from subatomic particles to societies. In Chapter 1, we'll go inside high-energy accelerators to explore the cusp at which energy turns to matter, a process called "resonance hunting." From small and simple examples, we'll uncover the principles of resonance that apply equally to large-scale change. Combining wisdom from the West and the East, we'll see how they resolve and complement in showing us both how resonance works and how it can work *through us*. Chapter 2 will further look at resonance at the human level of mind and body. We'll see how "getting on the same wavelength" with others is not mere metaphor, but a felt experience with measurable effects. We'll refresh on the neurobiology that supports social resonance, recognizing "mind", *a la* Dan Siegel, as an "embodied, relational process that directs the flow of energy." We'll see how the mind can take in universal energy and concentrate it through the physical matter of the body. We'll also see the power of resonating as a highly cohesive, integrated being, and why none of us can take that as a given, which sets up our work in Part II.

In Part II we'll explore how to become a more resonant being, starting with a Zen toolkit of useful practices. In Chapter 3, we'll go inside the metaphorical ACME box to look at how to integrate those pieces rolling around in the bottom using one breath, two-sided thinking, three energy centers, and four patterns in the nervous system. We'll learn why mindfulness of thoughts or emotions alone is not sufficient to get our mind-body system resonating more clearly. Rather we need embodied practices to re-tune the slower changing scaffolding of the body in order for it to support a different quality of thought and emotion. Chapter 4 will explore how to tune our human-musical-instrument using the vibration of sound and other means to free the internal tension that otherwise dulls us. We'll then turn in Chapter 5 to taming the "mind of its own" that our system came with, pre-programmed for its own survival. Stuck in the past, fearing for itself, thinking too small, our ego self may never realize the purposes it could be put to. We'll see that Zen training resolves the false sense of separation between our local ego self and our whole universal Self. What emerges through this re-connecting with our true nature is the wisdom of connectedness, by which we increasingly resonate with the energy around us—i.e., universal energy—and conduct what matches us through our daily deeds. We'll discover that nothing feels more purposeful or perfect than when we're able to function this way: as an instrument of the Way.

This opens up a world of resonant possibility, which is the topic of Part III. From love and relationships, to leadership and work, to large-scale social change, we explore how we can use ourselves as well-tuned, co-creating instruments of change. We'll look at the neuroscience of relationships and how we can resonate in a way that gets people moving with us. We'll explore how to use resonance to remove fear and make relationships more loving and less conflicted (Chapter 6). We'll show how to realize goals and co-create with greater effectiveness and less effort using "driving rhythm," which is a kind of "resonance hunting" on the human scale and moves us into the realm of leadership (Chapter 7). We'll see how leadership builds resonance and brings about flow within a team or organization, and how it really is possible for the whole to be greater than the sum of its parts (Chapter 8). And finally, we'll explore the four ingredients needed for large-scale change based on the principles of resonance (Chapter 9), and what's present or missing in our efforts to address issues such as coronavirus or climate change.

Because here's the long and short of it and where we'll wind up in Chapter 10: whatever difference you make in this world will happen through resonance. That difference may last for a lickety-split second, a lifetime, or leave a legacy, depending on how well you resonate with the larger forces around you, how much you conduct universal energy through your thoughts, words and deeds. To live, love and lead in accord with universal energy is to accord the Way in the truest sense. It's not easy, and yet leads to the greatest ease. And it may just be that this book crossing your path is no more of an accident than Tre Wee sending me an email. It may be that you're already primed to resonate with what you pick up in these pages, and use it to expand into greater love, purpose, and possibility. You'll come away with insight into how resonance works, concrete practices to resonate more fully through an integrated mind-body-as-one, and practical ways to apply your more-resonant self to how you live and make your difference. Here you've already opened the big cardboard box and pulled out this magnificent Universal Energy Concentrator. What else is as worthy of your attention as figuring out how to use it?

Not to mention, the times demand it.

PART I

RESONANCE DOES EVERYTHING

Where it becomes clear that resonance creates form,
destroys form, and is the principle of change itself

I

ENERGY AND MATTER

He had bright eyes, Bernd did, and no shortage of energy. He sought me out during the networking hour before dinner on the last night of our four-day leadership program. From the program's beginning, we'd been exploring ways to thrive in a disruptive, complex, accelerating world, probably not unlike the world you live in. Bernd, who led a countrywide sales team, was living disruption close-up and personally, as he'd just learned that his division had been sold off to another company. I expected he wanted to talk through his situation or vent his frustration.

"How do I continue practicing?" he asked, in reference to an introductory meditation session I had offered at lunchtime. "And where can I learn more about meditation?" His curiosity brought him to a program at our Institute for Zen Leadership (IZL), which launched him into a daily meditation practice. He started feeling more whole, less separate. "It's showing up in everything I do," he wrote a few weeks after the program. "Swimming feels more whole, driving feels more whole, talking and interacting with others feels more whole. I like it!" Such is the feeling of resonating one-with the energies around us: we feel more a part of, not apart from, the people and processes of daily life.

Still, Bernd's daily life was plenty challenging as he was faced with shutting down his group due to the acquisition. How could he help his people land? What would he do? It was clear he'd be out of a job. These are conditions that would make many people hyper and anxious, yet Bernd did the opposite: he slowed down, and he continued his meditation. In the midst of frightened, nervous people, Bernd must have felt like an oasis in the desert. People kept seeking him out. "I don't feel like I'm running so fast," he wrote me in the thick of it. "I'm more aware of the feelings of others. In fact, my boss was worried that I might be looking too relaxed and people would think I'm not working hard enough. I had to laugh; I'm getting more done than ever." His slower pace even served him financially. While colleagues were anxiously accepting early buy-out offers from the acquiring company, Bernd waited patiently. In the end, he received a much more generous severance package. Such is the resilience of resonating with the Way.

I start with an end in mind, as I hope through these pages you find the way to your own version of Bernd's experience, where you feel more whole, less separate. Where you realize greater effectiveness with less effort. Where you can help the people around you by being one-with, not one-up. Where, in good times and bad, you can make the resounding difference that is yours to make. All of this is possible through resonance. In Part I, you'll learn the principles of resonance. In Part II, you'll learn how to embody them, and in Part III, how to apply them.

We'll launch our journey by exploring the principles of resonance in nature, in the dance of energy and matter. We'll look at this concept of universal energy from both Western and Eastern views to see where they converge and complement. From each we'll learn something crucial about how we can resonate true to our nature and bring about resonance in the world that strengthens our relationships, realizes our goals, and manifests our purposes. I should own up front that science really sings to me. If it doesn't sing to you, skim this part—you won't be lost later. But what I hope you can get a feel for in these opening pages is just how vast and remarkable is this sea of vibrating energy that you and I dance in. While we'll enter resonance through the science, you'll see it's also downright spiritual. To begin, let's ground what we're talking about in some everyday experiences of resonance.

CLEAR AS A BELL

Figure 1-1. Brass striker vibrates a bell

DING-g-g-g! The striker comes down on the round brass bell and its clear sound fills the room. Having trained in Zen for many years, that sound is primal for me, as it opens and closes each period of meditation. DING-g-g-g. The sound eases us into the start of meditation as we match the ring with a long, slow exhale. At the other end of a period of meditation—especially one of those long sits where we've been pushing to our limits—DING-g-g-g—it's the most welcome and beautiful sound on earth!

Whether you meditate or not, you've heard many bells a-ringing and you probably already know this is an example of resonance. At its most basic, to resonate is to "sound again," i.e., re-sound a signal or vibrate with something else. We can think of it as receiving an energetic signal and doing something with it or, conversely, sending out an energetic signal that gets picked up. The signal, in this case, comes from a brass striker landing on the bell. The laws of physics tell us that energy is neither created nor destroyed, but only transferred and transformed. As that pulse of energy is transferred to the bell, a small amount is dissipated in friction, and the rest sends a wave of energy through the bell, creating vibration. Because the bell is round, waves come around and reinforce one another, further vibrating air molecules, and add up to a pleasing sound: DING-g-g-g!

The possibility of signals adding up or getting amplified gives us a second, even richer meaning to resonate, which is when the energy that is received activates a new state: a system-wide effect where energy adds to something bigger. A bell can amplify sound due to its round shape, which is a kind of feedback loop. Other systems resound and amplify signals by bouncing them off a couple of endpoints (e.g., a guitar string), or with feedback loops among its parts (e.g., an electric guitar and amplifier). Resonance can also be amplified through repeated stimulation. I could make the bell sound last longer by striking it again and again.

Conversely, when connection or feedback in a system is broken, resonance dies quickly. This audibly hit home for me recently when one of our bells at the dojo was accidentally dropped on concrete. At first it looked fine, but the shock had made the tiniest crack through the brass. When the bell was struck, it gave out the deadest, dullest, "duh"—no resonance at all. The crack made it impossible for energy waves to add up.

I've simulated this effect in our IZL programs with groups of people standing in a circle holding hands. I start a wave by raising my right hand a few inches, which raises the left hand of my neighbor, who transfers that energy to her right hand, moving the left hand of the next person, and so on around the circle. The energy comes back around, each person does it again. As long as we're all following about the same jiggle rules, the energy keeps circulating and building. We're like a bell ringing (see Figure 1-2a). Now if we break our circle between two people, as soon as the wave gets to the first of them, their right hand movement just waves in the air and the next person never gets the signal. "Duh." (Figure 1-2b) The signal dies. Again, the energy doesn't truly disappear, it just changes form, but the systemwide wave is dead.

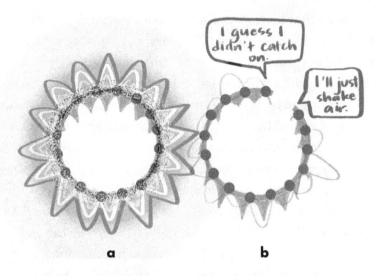

Figure 1-2. Resonance in an unbroken circle vs. a circle broken

A wave of movement energy can pass around a circle of people holding hands and keeps growing with every pass (a). If the circle is broken, resonance dies out after the first round (b).

Simple as it is, our bell is also choosy in what kind of energy it can use. A brass striker hitting a brass bell is an efficient way to generate a pulse of energy that travels through the bell. But, say a cosmic ray zipped through the room with the bell in its path. The bell has no way to use that frequency of energy. From the cosmic ray's point of view, it will simply pass through—nothing to do here. From the bell's point of view, it will ignore the cosmic ray. So, for resonance to occur, there has to be a match between the energy available to a system and its ability to use that energy. Energy that can't be used is sort of like junk mail; it doesn't get picked up.

Let's take it a step further. Say I tap my brass bell with a cotton ball. Some energy would be transferred, maybe enough to jiggle a bit of the bell, but not enough to activate a ring. Even though I'm sending some energy into the bell, it's not enough. So, even if a system is capable of resonating, systemwide resonance won't be apparent until we hit a certain threshold, or what Malcolm Gladwell popularized as a "tipping point." Tapping on my bell with a weak little cotton ball, I stay well below the tipping point to activate a ring, but I still impart a small amount of energy that dissipates, i.e., spreads out into greater disorder or entropy. Since the bell can't store that energy, we might say it's insignificant or wasted. But in systems that do have a way to store dissipated energy (for example, our atmosphere with its ability to store CO_2 and heat), latent effects can add up over time. What's tricky about latent change is that it builds gradually and invisibly before it appears suddenly, as the changing climate is now showing us.

As a final variation on ringing our bell, imagine we stuffed it full of cotton balls. We strike the bell and it's a little better than if it had a crack in it, but it's still dull and flat. Why? We can go back to our hand-holding people in the circle and imagine doing the whole exercise chest deep in a room full of cotton balls. Every time we'd move our hands, it would be so darn difficult with all that friction that the signal would be smaller, less effective, and die out sooner. So even a simple bell can only ring its true note—i.e., resonate fully—when it's whole and clear of obstructions. The same is true of you and me, which will inspire our work in Part II. That's why we say resonance is a physical fact, but how effectively we resonate is where we have choice.

We're getting ahead in our story, looking at personal and large-scale applications of resonance, but they help round out a definition for resonance as depicted in Figure 1-3 and summarized as follows: Resonance arises as energy is transferred. We say something resonates when it can vibrate with something else. From the point of view of the receiving system, we say it resonates when it can take in energy and do something with it—relay, change, or amplify it. From the point of view of the stimulating system, we say it resonates when its energy is transferred to something else. If the incoming energy doesn't match or there isn't enough of it, it either has no effect or it dissipates in or around the system, eventually getting cancelled out or stored as latent energy that might add up later.

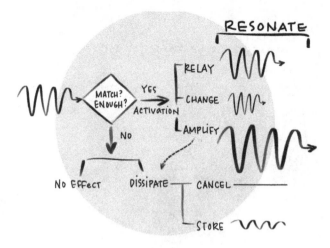

Figure 1-3. Resonate defined

We can look at a simple system like a bell to get a working definition of resonance and explore some of its principles. But even more interesting possibilities emerge when one thing leads to another and waves upon waves add up to sometimes surprisingly big effects.

WAVES UPON WAVES

If you pluck a guitar string, it vibrates at a particular frequency and wavelength that we associate with a musical note. We hear the amplitude of those waves as volume. These three terms—frequency, wavelength, and amplitude—characterize energy of all kinds (see Figure 1-4). Frequency is the number of waves per unit time (1 wave/second = 1 Hz), while wavelength is the distance between peaks. You could say they describe the rhythm of the energy in time (frequency) and space (wavelength). They're also interrelated: the higher the frequency, the shorter the wavelength. Amplitude tell us the height of the peaks; i.e., the amount of that energy. So, for example, if I want a higher frequency note on a guitar, I shorten the string's wavelength of vibration by pressing on a fret. If I want a louder note, I pluck the string harder or, for an electric guitar, turn up the gain on its amplifier.

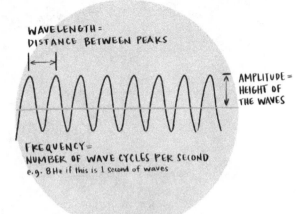

Figure 1-4. Frequency, wavelength and amplitude of waves

Energy is characterized by its frequency and wavelength. Frequency describes its rhythm in time, i.e., cycles per second, while wavelength describes its repetition over space, i.e., distance between peaks. Amplitude describes the amount of this energy, i.e., volume.

Now picture a great iron and concrete bridge spanning a gorge. You'd think, being made of strong, solid stuff, it would be stable. But like a big guitar string, it, too, is capable of vibrating end-to-end. Ordinary traffic wouldn't be enough energy to activate this end-to-end vibration (though you've probably felt how bridges vibrate under heavy traffic). But on a particular day in 1940, the winds whistling through the Tacoma Narrows reached such a tipping point. Like a string plucked, the entire Tacoma Narrows Bridge started vibrating end-to-end and soon tore itself apart[1]. For the same reason, soldiers are instructed to break step when crossing a bridge because their synchronized footsteps could match a resonant frequency of the bridge with enough energy to take it down. Teasing apart what's happening in these examples, we'll see how waves upon waves of energy can add up.

We'll start with the soldiers' footsteps because that's easier to picture. As depicted in Figure 1-5a, we could think of a solider as a little wave of footstep energy—E1—landing on the bridge at a marching frequency of one step/second (i.e., 1 Hz). Let's say the bridge has a resonant frequency of half that, so every other step matches a rate at which the bridge can vibrate. But it takes a lot more than the energy of one marcher to activate that system-wide effect. We'll call Eb the threshold or tipping point at which the whole bridge starts vibrating.

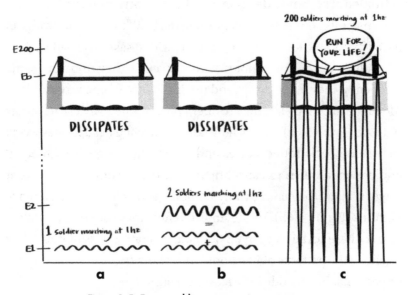

Figure 1-5. Energy adding up to activate resonance

If we now add a second identical soldier doing exactly the same march, we get double the energy—E2—landing on the bridge every second. This shows us how "getting on the same wavelength" can add up, increasing the amplitude of energy (Figure 1-5b). But E2 is still well below Eb and the bridge isn't moving. But now say we have 200 soldiers marching and, every second, an "E200" amount of energy is landing on the bridge. Now the amplitude of the soldiers' wave is so great it exceeds Eb (Figure 1-5c). Big waves of jiggling molecules spread out every second and, before they can dissipate, they're bouncing back from the other end of the bridge, adding up to more internal energy, and matching a frequency at which the bridge as a whole is able to vibrate. With enough energy of a matching frequency, system-wide resonance is activated.

Even though wind is a more chaotic waveform, the same principle was at work the day the winds were strong enough to trigger the Tacoma Narrows Bridge collapse. Normal wind hitting the bridge might be likened to a cotton ball striking our bell—well below the activation of system-wide resonance. But the forty mph winds that day were more like our brass striker hitting the bell, "ringing" the bridge in a way it was able to move—in this case, with disastrous results.

When waves come upon waves, even if they're of the same frequency, they don't always add up. If the "up" of one wave hits the "down" of another—i.e., they're out of phase—they cancel each other out (see Figure 1-6a). This is how noise-canceling headphones work; they sense background noises and match those signals with equal and opposite waves to cancel them out. If two somewhat different waves collide, they create more complex waves having interference patterns (Figure 1-6b). While "interference" may sound undesirable, in fact, these patterns open up boundless creative possibilities. They might be the patterns of harmonies in a choir, chords on a keyboard, or patterns that encode information (Figure 1-6c).

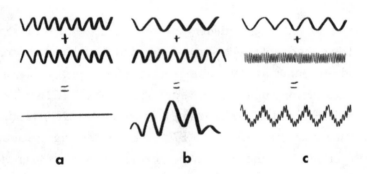

Figure 1-6. Waves canceling out, interfering, encoding information

When sound waves, for example, interfere with or modulate higher frequency carrier waves, they can be transmitted long distances and decoded by a receiving antenna, which is how broadcast radio works. Those high frequency carrier waves are in the room where you are right now, but you don't hear them because, again, resonance is specific and while you have antenna for sound waves (i.e., ears), you don't have antenna for the much higher frequency carrier wave, so it goes right past you. But if you hooked up a radio having such an antenna, you'd have proof that those waves are surely present.

Interference patterns can be downright beautiful, as in an orchestra. Just as a bell sounds different than a guitar, so every instrument of an orchestra has its own resonant quality. When all instruments are playing the same note, for example when they're tuning to the A-note at the beginning of a performance, you can hear the sound of "A" getting louder and clearer as more waves join the party and add to the amplitude of "A" energy, but it's not particularly interesting. Far more interesting is what happens as each instrument starts playing its own line of a musical score. Combinations of wave-notes create major and minor chords, and the rate and quality at which different instruments play create patterns within patterns that add up to the magnificence of a Beethoven symphony—something no single instrument could do on its own. This shows us that the way waves add up is not limited to identical soldiers marching in lockstep, but can be a highly creative combination of different instruments getting on "the same page" of music, or aligned by a common purpose.

Often, as waves upon waves come together, so much starts happening at the same time we call it chaos. For example, out my window I can see waves upon waves on Round Bay, which is a widening of the Severn River feeding the Chesapeake Bay and Atlantic Ocean. Two boats go by of different size, casting different wakes that merge, creating new waves and chop. And here comes a zippy jet ski, crossing them both creating interference patterns where some waves pop up, others die down. The prevailing wind of the day activates an overall wave pattern across the water, and now a gust of wind creates a ripple across the top of all the waves. A fish pops up, evidenced by a tiny series of circular waves spreading out from where it broke the surface.

If we were to examine any area of water in Round Bay right now, we'd see it resonating with many waves simultaneously and gradually dissipating them, sending them to the shoreline where their energy dissipates into waving grasses or craggy rocks. Some patterns encode information. For example, a discerning sailor would know a high frequency ripple across the top of waves indicates a local gust worth steering toward. The overall pattern of waves changes moment by moment and defies prediction, yet arises through the deeper order of waves upon waves. It's also hard to establish causality because as waves come upon waves, both are changed as they vibrate together. When I strike a bell, it's easy to pick out subject and object. But when a jet ski zips by, it is both an object bounced around by the waves already there and a subject making more waves. What this snippet of Round Bay shows us is that real world systems are complex, chaotic, able to absorb and resonate with many energies simultaneously, and are constantly changing as more energies arrive or dissipate[2].

In this sea of complexity, it would be impossible to try to analyze or predict which wave will have which effect. But we can use the specificity and effects of resonance to get our answers. Even though a system might be able to resonate with many frequencies and we have no idea what they are, when we find one that matches, the system will tell us. For example, if I shout into the strings of a grand piano, the strings that match the vibrations in my voice will start vibrating because they can use some of that energy. They won't be as loud as if they'd been hit with a hammer, but they'd be vibrating. And those that don't match my voice will be doing nothing. As another example, if I play middle C on the piano, other C-strings will also start subtly vibrating because they're a multiple of the same frequency—i.e., harmonics—so they can use some of middle C's energy and resonate with it. Meanwhile, the B's and D's remain silent.

This leads us to a crucial insight about working with resonance. Since resonance naturally reveals itself in the buildup of energy, it opens up new ways for us to work that rely more on sensitivity and adjustment than on prediction and plans. We'll use this feature a great deal in Part III as we look at applications. But do these principles of resonance really apply beyond the wavy world of sound, water, and the occasional bridge? How prevalent is resonance and how general are these insights we've uncovered? To get our answers, we have to look a bit deeper.

RESONANCE HUNTING

Walking down the hallway of the physics building in college, I caught sight of a sign above one of the office doors: High Energy Physics. I had no idea what that meant, but I knew that I wanted it. I went inside and was relieved to find a professor in that department who I already knew. I started working in Dr. Ma's lab that week. Physics was my first science love because I was fascinated with energy. What I especially loved about high energy physics was that it studied the in-between—the cusp where energy turns to matter, matter back into energy. As your guide into this high energy world, I'll try not to get us lost in details, but it really ties everything together for me, and I would love for it to do the same for you.

Let's start with energy in everyday life. Sound is an example of energy waves at the lower end of what's called the electromagnetic spectrum, vibrating around 10-20000 Hz. These waves resonate with many things in our material world, including air molecules, musical instruments, our eardrums and bodies. At opposite end of the electromagnetic spectrum lie high frequency waves such ultraviolet (UV), X-rays, and gamma rays. In between is a narrow band of vibrations we call visible light. Energy in this range vibrates cells in our eyes that resound in our brains as waves that we interpret as images. It also vibrates with matter in our world, where some frequencies are absorbed, others reflected, giving us a world most of us see in living color.

Looking closely at any one of these light-striking interactions, we'd see it has the same specificity as shouting into the strings of a piano.

The frequency of light has to match something in the system it lands on for the two to vibrate together. Einstein, for example, showed that red light hitting a kind of photographic surface had no effect, but higher frequency UV light could vibrate electrons right out of their orbit, the so-called Photovoltaic Effect (for which he was awarded the Nobel Prize). Of course, we don't see light energy vibrating the way we can see a guitar string vibrating because it happens so much faster than our brains can process. Our brainwaves operate in the meager range of 30 Hz, while visible light is vibrating 100,000,000,000,000 times faster than that. Just like a propeller turning rapidly appears to us as a solid disc, so high frequency vibrations appear to us as a solid stream.

This is really important—that rapid vibrations appear solid to us—because it accounts for our conventional misconceptions about the lively activity underlying what appears to be stillness. Our misconceptions become even more dense when we start talking about matter. Conventionally, we'd say matter comes in several states: solid, liquid and gas. Since the ancient Greeks, we've taken matter apart to try to get at the basic building blocks of the universe, what the Greeks called atoms, meaning "indivisible." But this turned out to be quite the misnomer, as not only was the atom divisible, but even its parts—such as protons—were found to be not just particles, but also rapidly vibrating waves.

Pause on that for a moment, that subatomic particles also have a wave nature—what's called wave-particle duality. It's mind-blowing to a conventional, Western view of the world based on taking things apart to understand them. Wave properties can be lost when you take systems apart (imagine how many waves I'd lose in Round Bay if I chopped it up into ice-cube trays). Moreover, waves are darned interesting. A particle can be here or there; a wave can be both here *and* there. Waves have more spread-out effects that may be partly manifest and partly hidden. How ironic that a deep enough search for universal building blocks would end in waves.

So matter and energy are actually not all that different, which is pretty much the point of Einstein's famous $E=mc^2$. Matter (i.e., stuff that has mass, m) is none other than a concentrated form of energy, E, related by the very big number that is the speed of light squared. Both energy and matter have a wave-like nature. Both vibrate, indeed matter vibrates at an even higher frequency than electromagnetic energy, so no wonder it looks solid, even relative to light. Going back to our spinning propeller, if it were vibrating at the frequency of a proton, it would be rotating more than a billion times faster than light. Amidst all that vibration, it takes on a quality called mass that is drawn to other masses by a force known as gravity.

Having connected energy and matter, Einstein worked mightily to find a unifying principle behind electromagnetism and gravity. He didn't find this so-called unified field theory, but his quest was taken up by many others. It led to high energy accelerators such as at CERN and Fermilab, and the field of high energy physics that so enchanted me. Smashing particles together and creating energetic conditions not seen since the Big Bang, these accelerators have revealed fundamental wave-particles that aggregate into the forms of our world. The hunt for these wave-particles is sometimes called "resonance hunting" because they only appear at certain energetic frequencies. What has emerged is a standard model of fundamental wave-particles that looks sort of like a mini periodic table of elements, except it's characterizing not atoms, but what makes up atoms, as well as other forms of energy[3]. It includes classes of what are called quarks, leptons and force carriers[4], including the Higgs boson, dubbed by the popular press as the "God particle"—evidence of how this search for fundamentals starts seeming downright spiritual.

String Theory is the most complete unified field theory tying all this together, if you will, whereby the properties of these wave-particles emerge as resonant frequencies of infinitesimal loops of vibrating strings. To use a musical metaphor, if I hit three keys on a piano—C-E-G—their wave forms vibrate together to produce a chord we hear as C-major. Likewise, as Brian Greene writes in *The Elegant Universe*:

> Rather than producing musical notes [like a piano string], each of the preferred patterns of vibration of a string in string theory appears as a particle whose mass and force charges are determined by the string's oscillatory pattern . . . Far from being a collection of chaotic experimental facts, particle properties in string theory are the manifestation of one and the same physical feature: the resonant patterns of vibrations[5].

So, an up-quark is a string vibrating one way, a down-quark is vibrating another way. Put two up-quarks and a down-quark together with a gluon (no shortage of quirky names in this field) and you get a chord vibrating as a proton. Put chords of protons, neutrons and electrons together and you get atoms. Put atoms together and you get the music of solids, liquids, gases, brass bells, cotton balls, you and me, along with plants, animals, families, communities, and civilizations. All the way up and down this chain, every form is made up of smaller vibrations and every vibration contributes to a larger form. Vibrating energy within vibrating energy.

So if everything is vibrating energy of one form or another, think of the vast implications for resonance. When energies meet, if one can use what the other provides, then energy transfers. From the point of view of the receiving system, we say it resonates by relaying, changing or amplifying what it receives. From the point of view of the stimulating system, we say it resonates because its energy was picked up and used. From a bird's eye view, we say the two systems resonated because they vibrated with one another and both were changed. In other words, resonance is how energy changes form. And since everything is a form of energy, it's *how change happens*. It's universal.

That's not to say this micro-level vibrational analysis is the most *practical* way to explain all change. We have many other physical and social sciences that better describe change at macro-levels—from meteorological predictions of weather to biological descriptions of evolution. But that doesn't mean this fundamental energetic level stops working or that wave-particles stop vibrating. Indeed, because everything comprises vibrations within vibrations, it's often quite useful to consider how system-level vibrations show up in everyday life. For example, we wouldn't analyze the change evoked in a fender bender by looking at vibrating protons; we'd just want to know who hit whom and what's the damage. But we may find it useful to feel into the rhythm or frequency of traffic when merging onto an expressway so we can better avoid collisions. We wouldn't invoke sympathetic vibrations to understand how wood turns to ash in a fireplace. But we would find it useful when starting a fire to find the right frequency of blowing air onto the early sparks to get them to catch. The more we get a feel for a world of matter and energy as nested vibrations, the more we sense how rhythms emerge in our everyday life and, better yet, how to work with them.

Before leaving String Theory, there's another dimension of it worth mentioning, namely that it describes a universe of mind-blowing dimensions. Generally, we can think in only the three dimensions of our material world: length, width and depth. We can sort of get our heads around time as a fourth dimension. But even our notions of space and time as being fixed were upended by Einstein, who showed them to be conventions within a frame of reference. String Theory points to a universe of *ten dimensions*. What the heck are the other six? According to Universe Today[6], the fifth dimension is an axis of separation from our current reality and the sixth dimension is a plane of other possible worlds going backwards and forwards in time. By the tenth dimension, "everything possible and imaginable is covered." Now, mind you, these are not mere fantasies, but terms needed in the equations of a unified field theory to reconcile decades of high energy experiments and something as down to earth as gravity. So even though we can't grasp them like a brass bell, there is some grounding to the idea that future possibilities, for example, have some energetic signature in the present moment—a possibility that teachers like Joe Dispenza and Deepak Chopra claim to leverage with many stories of success[7].

So what is this unified field, or what I've been calling universal energy? We can think of it as the sum total of energies from all the forces we know (such as electromagnetism and gravity), plus energies we don't consciously perceive (such as gamma rays and the dense vibrations of matter), in dimensions we can measure on a ruler as well as those we can only access mathematically. The universe and all its energy is one fascinating place! It's also fascinating that Western science would come to describe this universe in terms of the ceaseless flex and flow of energy that is partly hidden and partly manifest, since, without all the details, this was pretty much where the Eastern view started from.

UNIVERSAL ENERGY

Around the time the Greeks were breaking down the universe to understand it in terms of basic building blocks, halfway around the world the Chinese were articulating principles of the same universe from the opposite direction: what made it whole? And how can one live in harmony with this whole? While the ideas articulated in the *Tao Te Ching* were already present in Chinese culture, their compilation, attributed to Lao Tzu ("Old Master") around 300 BCE, resonated so deeply with people that it has been translated, studied, and applied in every generation since.[8] While in the West, "Tao" is often misinterpreted as a "thing"—as some kind of Frist Principle or pre-ordained path—the masterful translation by Roger Ames and David Hall gives us a more dynamic, Eastern understanding of the ceaseless process they call "Way-making." *Tao Te Ching* literally translates as the Classic ("Ching") of this Focus ("Te") and Its Field ("Tao"). Ames and Hall, underscoring the human project this work addresses, pull out its more intentional meaning in their subtitle: "Making This Life Significant."[9]

In terms of resonance, we could say Way-making is an emergent relationship between a particular resonator ("Te") and its field ("Tao"). When we, as that particular resonator, work in harmony with the field around us, we naturally vibrate with certain people, conditions and opportunities, and what comes into focus through us is exactly the significance of our being in that field. Put another way, because nothing exists in isolation, including us, our energies either match or don't match the field around us. The most efficacious process of Way-making or living according to the Way ("Tao" in Chinese, "Do" in Japanese) is to match, to move naturally with the flow and balance of energies, whereby we are non-contentious co-creators[10]. Way-making does not require we engage in the frantic scramblings of an "I" trying to make a difference. Rather it moves with the principle of *wu-wei*— doing without an "I" trying to do, as in: "Way-making emulates what is spontaneously so."[11]

In a world of ceaseless change, nothing exists statically, but instead is always in the process of coming or going, rising or falling, and ever containing its opposite. From absolute emptiness arises the Chi (Japanese: Ki) of the universe, or what we're calling universal energy. The dynamism of Chi is expressed as co-arising opposites, represented in the yin-yang symbol. These energies not only flow into one another, but also intrinsically contain one another; the little black circle within the white represents the hidden within the manifest. If we were to view this symbol edge-on and depict the white as what's seen "above the waterline" and the black as hidden "below the waterline," we could imagine the wave form it represents (see Figure 1-7). This up-and-down nature of energy creates vibration, and vibrations within vibrations give rise to the many forms of our world.

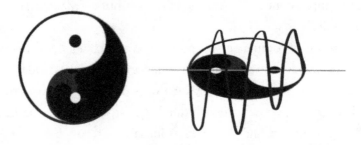

Figure 1-7. Yin and Yang as a waveform

Taoism represents the Way of the universe as a sort of 2-dimensional oscillation of yin and yang energy, where each contains the other. Viewed edge-on, it can be seen as vibrating energy that is partly manifest (peaks) and partly hidden (troughs).

The *Tao Te Ching* elucidates a way of "leading forth" in this world that is neither passive nor controlling, a way that is able to co-create without contention. For example, leaders who accord the Way do not over-assert their power, so people feel that they accomplish things themselves. The creations of Way-making artisans look like products of nature, without flourish or contrivance. Common sense regarding the Way is a shared awareness among common people of how universal harmony can be applied in their daily lives—from family relationships to farming fields.

Way-making functions in every energetic field we're a part of, and since we are never apart from an energetic field, we are always making way for better or worse. But when we sense that energy and act accordingly, we live more fortunate and significant lives. In Chinese culture, the fire-breathing dragon came to represent this universal energy and became a symbol of good luck. Of course, luck wasn't in the symbol, but in what was symbolized: being able to bring universal energy through oneself and become a dragon. When I speak of according the Way with a capital "W," it is this supreme naturalness I am referring to. There is nothing forced about resonating who we truly are or resonating with the energy that is naturally ours to work with.

Earlier we defined what it means to resonate in a Western science way, looking at an isolated bell receiving an isolated tap. An Eastern view reminds us that there are no truly isolated systems (indeed, we wouldn't even hear the bell without the surrounding air). Waves upon waves are ever-present and inter-penetrating. When patterns match between systems, vibrations add up and resonance occurs. Human beings in this sea are like our brass bell; some are clear, some are clogged, some are broken. When clogged or broken, they dissipate more energy than they're able to amplify. Healing what's broken and taking away the extra, we arrive at what's essential—a true clear bell—that, without effort, will naturally vibrate its true, clear note when energetic conditions match. In turn, our vibration changes the constellation of vibrations around us in the systems we're a part of, relaying a true, clear note into this sea that will naturally stimulate vibration in others who match. From this connected view, the relational quality of resonance becomes even more evident: it is to vibrate *with*. And energies are ever-present that we can match or not-match.

Both Western and Eastern views provide crucial pieces to the puzzle of how we resonate and create resonance. The Western view gives us an objective, dissectible understanding of how resonance works. The Eastern view gives us an integrated sense of how resonance works *through us*. The Western view gave rise to sciences that took matter apart to understand it, but uncovered a world of interpenetrating, vibrating energy at its roots. The Eastern view gave rise to philosophical and spiritual traditions based on connectedness and harmony—recognizing that we affect one another and the systems we're a part of, even when it's not apparent. The Western view gave rise to philosophical and spiritual traditions based on separation; a core story, for example in Western religion opens with individuals being thrown out of the Garden of Eden, and the subsequent human quest to reconnect with God. Whether we think of it as harmonizing with universal energy or reuniting with God or Spirit or however we name it, this move toward what

Ken Wilber calls "unity consciousness" is the very vector of human development—both West and East[12].

Wilber's Integral Theory further shows how both objective understanding (i.e., exterior) and subjective experience (interior) need to be included in any description of reality, and that neither reduces to the other[13]. Likewise both Western and Eastern approaches give us necessary and irreducible insight into resonance. The West developed a view of energy centered "out there" as something to be studied through such disciplines as physics. The East gave us an understanding of energy centered "in here" as something to be cultivated through such practices as meditation, Tai Chi, yoga, Aikido, and other traditions. Western science has shown us that energy is neither created nor destroyed but is forever changing form. The East has given us traditions such as Zen where one can directly experience connectedness and the truth of "emptiness is form, form is emptiness." The Western view helps us understand resonance objectively; Eastern practices help us embody it subjectively. It's a good thing that humanity took two different roads to understanding the universe, and that we live at a time when we can use both. Especially since, in the West, we severed science from spirituality several centuries ago and are only now beginning to find ways to let them catch up with each other.

As a Western scientist long before I became a Zen teacher, I feel obliged to say a few more words about universal energy, because I know it can sound abstract and spiritual. And in a way, it *is* abstract and spiritual, because the complexity of our universe is simply beyond what we can grasp concretely. We have sense consciousness for just a tiny part of the electromagnetic spectrum. There's a whole spectrum of energy above and below what we consciously sense, all of which could carry information and be stimulating us in ways we're not conscious of. We're also not conscious of vibrations beyond a certain range. Our eyes can detect a flicker up to about forty Hz, but even a lightbulb running on a fifty to sixty Hz power source (which means it's pulsing on and off at that frequency), is smoothed into a solid stream of light by the limits of our perception. Most of the energy and all of the matter of our universe is vibrating faster by many orders of magnitude, creating co-vibrations we see only the occasional results of. We are, in a sense, sampling a movie playing much faster than our sampling rate, so we miss a lot. On top of all that, we experience only three or four dimensions of a ten-dimensional universe. How humbling to imagine all that we cannot imagine!

In Western science terms, universal energy embraces all of this: the manifest and hidden possibilities of the unified field, the entire electromagnetic spectrum from sound waves to gamma rays. It includes the light that makes these words visible, the thoughts they stimulate, the condensed energy that is the chair you're sitting on, and the more ethereal energy that is the spirit of the times. All are forms of energy, and resonance is the underlying principle to their changing forms.

In an Eastern sense, universal energy is this universe of energy in which we participate and what's universal in all of us: the active ingredient informing and animating all things. We might also call it God's love, the breath of Spirit, the Chi of the universe, or even speak to its fundamental source: God, Spirit, formless One, or absolute emptiness. At this level, all words are but poor approximations laden with cultural bias, but the subjective experience of resonating with this universal energy is available to humans, and has been taught and cultivated for thousands of years. Moreover, the human spirit, e.g., the energy of you as a particular, differentiated human being, comes to greatest fruition when it accords that which is also universal. I'll refer to this as according the Way; others might call it God's plan, one's destiny or fate. But resonance shows us that it's an off-road Way, a planless plan, an unfinished story, laid down in part by history and proactively co-created moment by moment. We are like the zippy jet ski crossing the wakes of other boats, vibrated by the waves already there, bouncing in ways characteristic to our making, and making a wake of our own. What we resonate with subtly changes us, even as we change the pattern of vibrations in this abundant sea of energy around us. How does all this energy come through the mind and body of human being? We turn to that next.

RESONANCE RECAP—ENERGY AND MATTER

- To resonate is to re-sound a signal, to receive energy and do something with it. It is to vibrate with.
- Resonance is universal: everything is energy. Even matter is a condensed form of energy, and energy ceaselessly changes form.
- Resonance is specific: it is a relational quality arising when energies match.
- Resonance is amplified and lasts longer through feedback loops and repeated stimulation.
- Dissipated energy is often regarded as noise or "wasted," but sometimes adds up to a tipping point.
- Resonance is a way of working with complex systems without prediction because it reveals itself when energies match.
- Universal energy is the totality of all waves of energy available. When we accord the Way, we are harmonizing with universal energy.

2

MIND AND BODY

pollo 14 astronaut Edgar Mitchell was the sixth man to walk on the moon, but he would tell people on his return that he brought back something even more important than moon rocks. On the trip back toward earth, he had just finished his shift of tasks and was gazing out the window. The Apollo capsule was slowly tumbling, revealing a carousel of images: sun, earth, moon, stars. And again: sun, earth, moon, stars. Suddenly he was overcome with a sense of expansion, where every molecule in his body was at one with what we saw. His senses fully alert, his mind took in the magnificence of this spiritual epiphany, this Samadhi experience. Profoundly at peace, one with the universe, the words he could bring to it were: "we are stardust."[14] But as is often the case when we have profound subjective experiences, he struggled to find others who could understand him, or how this experience fit into conventional science. Not having experienced anything similar, most people wanted to dismiss what he was telling them as a fluke, a curious state of mind, not a revelation of reality. But an unshakeable truth had penetrated and, on his return, Mitchell founded the Institute of Noetic Sciences to explore how spiritual experience could inform science and technology.

In talking about mind and body, we have to cross the same divide Edgar Mitchell struggled with between the subjective experience of mind, and an objective world shared by others. The body is an objective fact—a mix of energy and matter, while the mind is a subjective, energetic process that uses the body to create itself and its sense of the world. We often think of mind and body as two different things, but they are simply two aspects of the same phenomenon: resonance. The body takes in energy, changing its energetic forms, from which emerge the subjective experience we call mind, which in turn changes the flow of energy. We are in constant resonance with the energies around us and flowing through us, i.e., universal energy. To what extent is the mind universal vs. particular, i.e., tied to this particular body? To what extent is the body universal vs. tied to this particular life it has lived up till now? These important questions take us to the cusp of spirituality and science that Edgar Mitchell would have us explore. Because when we resonate at our best, this particular body is capable of having an experience of universal mind, and the wisdom emerging from that connectedness changes what the body does and how it does it.

In this chapter, we dig into how resonance works in mind and body, because that is the story of how we change, how we make a difference, and how we get others moving with us. On the one hand, the capacity of the body to vibrate with universal energy opens up vast possibilities. On the other hand, our embodiment of trauma, stressors and self-limiting habits can deaden our resonance and gives us work to do if we want to resonate fully. We'll review what's known about our multiple brains, energy centers, and mind-body patterns in the nervous system, and how each adds to our resonance when we function with mind-body-as-one. Since none of us would exist without relationships, we'll also see that the body is rife with social circuitry, and that we can measurably affect the body of others through the mind's intentions. All of this leads to an expanded view of mind that is both embodied and relational, both personal and universal, making the mind-body our very own Universal Energy Concentrator.

EATING ENERGY

I followed the trail of energy into graduate school. If high energy physics taught me that everything is energy and resonance is how energy changes form, I wanted to know: how does this show up in the human being? Mysterious Kirlian photography of human auras had emerged from Russia and I was fascinated that we might be able to study energy at the level of a whole person. In my graduate school applications, I wrote that much had been learned about the matter of living systems, but I wanted to study their energy. That was a pretty far out idea at the time, but the University of Chicago bought it, and I entered their Biophysics Department.

I didn't learn one bit about human auras, but I did learn a great deal about how life organizes itself. Ilya Prigogine had just been awarded the Nobel Prize for his work explaining how, in a world that is generally winding down toward greater entropy, life keeps winding up toward greater order. Life, Prigogine showed, is what's known as a dissipative system, one that metabolizes energy to evolve its order.[15]

To put it simply: we eat energy. We stay alive by finding energy we can use and change, relay or amplify, which is our definition of resonance. We don't normally think of metabolism as an example of resonance because we study such processes at a more macro-level (like organic chemistry) to explain how, for example, glucose gets metabolized. We don't tend to explain chemical reactions in terms of micro-level vibrations any more than we would explain a fender bender that way, but that doesn't mean those vibrations have stopped. Rather, they're exactly what underlies the specificity of those reactions; only certain things can vibrate together. Again, these vibrations are much faster than we can see, but like nested Russian dolls, they support larger-scale vibrations or rhythms we do see, from guts that rhythmically digest food, to hearts that beat, to muscles that move our lungs, to the frequency of our walk as we head into the kitchen to periodically eat and keep the whole cycle running. Vibrations within vibrations within vibrations.

Moreover, these vibrations evolve our order as human beings, from one cell to many, from infancy to adulthood. Every stage we grow into is the result of resonance, where we're metabolizing the energies of air, food, water, etc., along with life experience and relationships, pushing us to thresholds of increasing maturity. The idea that we can take in energies of future possibilities and manifest their forms in the present is nor far-fetched: we've been doing it all along.

But neither is that to say anything goes, because as we've seen, resonance is also specific. Different parts of our mind-body system vibrate with energy at different rates. If our mind-body were an orchestra, some parts would be like fast-trilling piccolos, while other parts are like a timpani drum. What this gives us is a mind-body that cannot change all at once or at the same rate.

THOUGHTS, EMOTIONS AND HABITS

As a gross but useful generalization, the different aspects of our mind-body system change more slowly as they move from being subtle energy to condensed matter. The energetic aspects of mind, such as thoughts and perceptions, change most rapidly. Effects mediated by fluids come next, followed by those changing the physical scaffolding of the body. For example, our energetic thoughts can play like the high-rate piccolo, jumping around and changing themes every few seconds as new inputs arrive. Once thoughts trigger emotions, hormones are dumped into our bloodstream, broadcast through our system, and endure for many minutes.[16] By contrast, it takes days to months for our nervous system to change its wiring, and it will only do so with repeated stimulation. And it takes weeks for muscles to build or bones to heal.

The good news, given these differing time scales of change, is that they make the body a stabilizing vehicle that can literally last a lifetime. The bad news is that we can get stuck in unproductive thought loops— i.e., states of mind—held in place by the slower changing body. One such loop happens between our thoughts and emotions (See Figure 2-1a). A perception, say, a fleeting glance from another person, gives rise to a thought—"She looked at me dismissively"—that triggers an emotion, say, anger and insecurity. Now chemicals have been dumped into our bloodstream that will take maybe twenty minutes to clear. Meanwhile, the body will keep sending signals back to the brain saying, in effect, "Send me more angry, insecure thoughts that reinforce this crappy feeling."

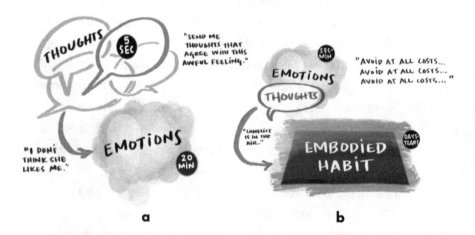

Figure 2-1. The thought-emotion loop and the habit-thought-emotion loop

Generally, the pace of changeability in the mind-body system decreases in moving from energetic thoughts to fluid-meditated emotions, to solid, embodied habits. While thought normally changes by the second, once emotions have been triggered, they can call up matching thoughts for maybe twenty minutes (a). Once a habit has been embodied, it can guide or constrain thoughts and emotions for days, weeks or years (b).

Conversely, positive emotions can set up positive resonant thought patterns, which is how affirmations work. "I expand into abundance, success and love every day and inspire those around me to do the same." With this affirmation, Gay Hendricks counsels readers of *The*

Big Leap to transcend self-limiting beliefs.[17] If we could watch what's happening in our bloodstream when this thought is strong and sincere, we'd see a different chemical flooding in, and a call up to the brain for more thoughts that agree with this big possibility. We'd also see the heart going into a smooth, coherent, variable rate of beating, (i.e., improved heart rate variability). In the presence of positive emotions, the heart beats differently, with measurable effects in our brain and on the electromagnetic field around our body.[18]

Likewise, movement of the physical body produces feedback loops to thoughts and emotions. For example, forming one's lips into a smile tends to produce a positive state of mind. Sharp punching and kicking movement produce feelings of aggression[19]. Even more enduring loops form when patterns of behavior get stored as habits in the physical body (Figure 2-1b). For example, when I was young, there was a good deal of conflict in our household, and I developed the habit of tip-toeing around or "walking on eggshells." That became a deeply embedded response in me so that even, years later, in cases where conflict really had to be tackled head-on, I'd shirk from it. Little wonder I was drawn to martial arts in college; I needed some serious retraining of my habits around conflict.

Benjamin Franklin would tell us that the key to a good life is good habits. The problem with habits—good or bad—is that they tend to desensitize us to the present and resonate with the past. Early in life, we started laying down habits before we had any control over our environment, or any awareness that we were laying down habits. Left on their own, habits from our childhood will continue to play out long after we're children and long after they're useful. As we get older, we deepen habits around how we work, play, eat, drink, handle stress, and so forth. It's easy to get addicted to stressful habits (and the chemicals they produce) and keep looping through more of the same. Only when we make unconscious habits conscious are we able to change them[20].

But just as with the thought-emotion loop, the relative endurance of patterns in the body can be good news if we use it to embody learning that we want to have operate reflexively, without even thinking about it. Whether it's 10,000 hours or 10,000 repetitions, we know mastery takes practice for a behavior or skill to get deeply embodied. But once embodied, it will function automatically. The lesson for how we resonate is that we do well to be choosy about the emotions we want to have linger and the habits we want to embody. And if we want to resonate effectively in the present, we have to build the habit of re-examining habits—something made all the more necessary given the bottom-up way we develop.

DEVELOPING FROM THE BOTTOM UP

It's now well-accepted that the brain developed in three major evolutionary stages and that how it develops in us as individuals mirrors the way it emerged in evolution. First came the primitive reptilian brain in the back of our heads, governing instinctual reactions. With the evolution of mammals came the midbrain, with its capacity for emotional reactions and connections. That's why we can have a two-way emotional connection with a dog that's simply not possible with a snake. As we keep climbing the evolutionary ladder and advancing in our development, we arrive to the expansion of the frontal cortex and its wide-ranging intellectual and executive functions.

But development of the nervous system actually starts lower down the evolutionary chain and physically lower in our own bodies. Even headless bacteria have simple systems for digesting food and regulating movement. Likewise in our body, nerves deep in our guts and spine develop first so we can digest food, register hunger and organize movement. Roughly a billion nerve cells line our guts, and dense clusters of motoneurons organize movement in our spine well before a sense of "I" emerges (i.e., the ego) around the age of two years. You can always tell when an ego boundary has formed because it comes with the onset of language. But in normal development, we learn to walk before we talk, which has important implications for this area of the lower abdomen, what in yogic traditions is associated with the lower two chakras and the Japanese call *hara*. This area organizes movement in the body and becomes our center of gravity; it gives us a sense of grounding and stability in the world. As any martial artist or sports person knows, engaging this area unleashes our greatest power. Moreover, if we can integrate *hara* into our overall orchestra, we get access to an intuitive consciousness that came before our sense of a separate self. We also get access to a manifesting power that can make stuff happen. We get our legs under us.

Once a living system gets to a certain size, it needs a way to get nutrients to all of its cells, and a heart starts beating to circulate food and oxygen. The heart, too, is a center of consciousness, sheathed by something close to 50,000 nerve cells, and regulated not only by nervous system connections, but also by our emotions, as meditated by hormones running through the very fluid it's pumping. Perhaps in part due to the sheer amount of blood in the heart, we register a felt sense of it being the center of emotions. But there's more to heartfelt emotions than that. When we're frustrated, anxious or worried, our heart rate variability (which is related to performance) shows jagged incoherence. When accompanied by positive emotions like gratitude and kindness, heart rate variability shows a smooth, coherent rhythm that can further entrain brain waves. Moreover, the massive pumping heart contributes to an electromagnetic field around our body that is 5,000 times stronger than that of the brain[21]. When heart and brain waves add up together, the effect is an amplification of our field that is measurable from across the room.

In yogic traditions, the heart is the fourth chakra, sitting at the intersection where top-down energies from "out there" meet up with bottom-up energies from "in here" organized by the will of the third chakra (the ego "I" at the solar plexus). Whether you look at the heart as a concentrator of emotions, a pivotal chakra, or an electromagnetic field generator, what's clear from studies at the Heart Math Institute, is that if we can integrate our heart into our overall orchestra, we resonate a much stronger signal into the world. Putting our whole heart into something is not only bringing emotional passion to it, but is also physically building resonance between the rhythmic waves of heart and brain.[22]

Finally, the head brain develops, in order from its most primitive to its most executive functions, partly as a way to converge competing signals from the rest of the body around what to do next. Our head brain contains around 100 billion nerve cells, each one capable of making thousands of connections. If we were to tease apart one of those nerve cells, we'd see it looks something like a tree (see Figure 2-2). It has many branches, i.e., dendrites, to receive stimulation from upstream sources. If it receives enough stimulation, the cell fires, resounding the signal through its "trunk," i.e., axon. In a sense, a nerve cell is similar to our bell in that it has to be hit with enough energy that matches what its dendrites can receive in order to resonate. If this were a sensory nerve sitting down in our spine, it might be picking up signals on our skin. If it were a motoneuron regulating movement, its axon would be stimulating a muscle. But if it's a nerve cell in our brain, it's generally connected to other nerve cells, often in a densely connected network.

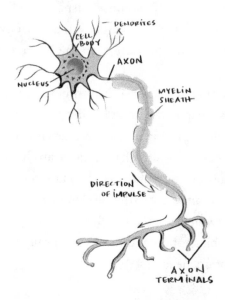

Figure 2-2. The resonator that is a nerve cell

A nerve cell receives signals at its branching dendrites and, if it receives enough stimulation— a neural "tipping point"—it relays that signal as an electrochemical pulse through its axon, in turn stimulating the cells it connects to.

Nerve cells in the brain, as well as throughout the body, become links in chain reactions that form neural pathways as we develop and learn. Refinement in these neural pathways again happens bottom-up; we go from a wobbly toddle to a reasonably stable walk before we learn how to control a crayon in our fingers. While new neural connections can be formed throughout our life—what's called neuroplasticity—they are especially being laid down and reinforced early in life. Repetition supports learning and habit formation in the nervous system: a neural pathway we use a lot gets more densely connected, making it easier to activate and more likely to be used again. As neuroscientist Gerald Edelman quipped, "What fires together wires together."

As the brain develops, it refines regions that map our body parts and coordinate movement. Not quite the top-down dictator we once imagined, the brain receives about nine times as many signals up from the body as it sends down[23]. It's also adding plenty of new information from head-based sensors. Starting from relatively primitive systems for processing the molecules of tastes and smells, it adds regions for making sense of sound and light energies. Just as the effects of emotion on our heart give us a felt sense of emotions residing in that area, so the concentration of senses, voice, and energetic sensations in the brain gives us a sense of the "I" of consciousness residing there, i.e., the "little voice in our head." While we know the subjective experience of mind derives from much more than the brain, this conventional assumption lingers.

The capabilities of the brain go further still. Even beyond what we think of as our five senses, deep in the brain lies the pineal gland containing tiny crystals capable of picking up high frequencies in the electromagnetic spectrum (beyond visible light), and transducing those signals into neuropeptides and hormones that regulate mood and behavior[24]. So even though the brain is last to the developmental party, it adds the capacity to resonate with new regions of the electromagnetic spectrum (and even the possibility of other dimensions), bringing in vast amounts of new information, head first.

The yogic tradition speaks to this top-down function in what it calls the descending or manifesting current. The fifth, sixth and seventh chakras are associated with throat, brow and crown of the head, respectively. From an Eastern view, we'd say the sixth chakra takes in universal energy flowing down from the seventh chakra, changes it into vivid imagery and other descending signals which are given voice and creative expression—i.e., made manifest—through the fifth chakra and below. The pineal gland is thought to be an excellent candidate for anchoring the energetic properties of the sixth chakra.

That said, there can be a risk in matching Eastern chakras with Western anatomical parts. Chakras emphasize subjective energy, while anatomy focuses on objective matter. But this is the same challenge we encounter in trying to equate the subjective experience of mind to an objectively measured set of brainwaves. We can say this subjective experience and that scientific measure seem to go together, but we can't say the experience is totally captured by the measure or that the measure causes the experience. In this respect, the chakra view is a useful bridge, because it gives us a way to see how material parts—such as the pineal gland—are also energetic centers. With the advent of such technologies as gas discharge visualization (GDV), energetic fields related to chakras are now objectively measurable[25]. The Eastern view can expand how we point our Western measuring devices, looking beyond the material gland, for example, to also study its electromagnetic effects. The more Western science has probed the energy of the body, the more it adds richness and detail to the Eastern view.

However we look at it, the brain, with its capacity for thought, language, memory, learning and imagination, contributes enormously to the mind's "I." Our subjective experience of mind emerges from this complex mass capable of resonating with so many energies running through it. The mind, in turn, is capable of resonating its experience into changes in the flow of energy in the brain, body, other people and physical world. As Dan Siegel puts it, "Mind is

an embodied, relational process that directs the flow of energy."[26]
But by the time it emerges in our development, ready to direct our
orchestra, our musicians have already been playing for a while. To
get our whole system playing together and continuing to evolve and
thrive, some of our metaphorical musicians will need re-training.

GROWING UP

Just as our body develops from the base, so we grow up through
stages of development that start primitive and evolve to higher order.
But the nervous system is wiring itself up all along, meaning we
embed habits at every stage that the next stage may have to partly
unwind. Children, once they form an ego boundary around the age
of two, operate in a largely ego-centric stage for the next several
years, experiencing the world as revolving around them. Seeing their
shadow, they might explain it as, "The sun is following me." Seeing a
toy, they'll be very clear if they want it ("Mine!"). Tasting a Brussels
sprout, they'll be very clear that they don't want it ("No!"). By the time
children develop empathy, usually in the range of five to nine years old,
and begin to sense what others are feeling, selfish habits will already
be in place. Do they share the ice cream with their friend or not? An
emerging maturity will say, "Share, and we'll both be happy," while
the voice of residual habit will say, "Forget it, the ice cream is mine!"

By the time we evolve to being rational, with facility using
logic, usually somewhere in our teens (though for some it's much
later or never happens), we already have a body wired with pre-
rational habits, such as my earlier example around conflict. My
other childhood strategy to deal with conflict was to throw myself
into schoolwork and try to do everything right. Somewhere along
the line, I came to the conclusion that if I did everything perfectly
my parents would argue less. Huh? Of course that wasn't the case,
but that's the kind of sense we make before we're old enough to
make sense. It set me up for a kind of perfectionism that would later

prove to be not only exhausting, but irritating to others—and never enough. These old and deep habits are particularly buried in the lower body, because that's what was maturing when they formed. All the more reason we focus on developing and integrating the *hara* to unwind this stuff and resonate more clearly with the present.

Even a reasonably healthy childhood produces a mind and body whose habits need re-examining to resonate optimally, yet life generally delivers a lot worse. Punch someone in the gut—physically or emotionally—and the gut muscles will reflexively tense. If life keeps delivering gut punches, eventually these muscles will hold residual tension and "forget" how to fully relax. If the trauma is particularly severe, dissociation happens—i.e., the person mentally "goes away" to create psychological distance from the trauma. This has the unfortunate effect of bypassing that part of the brain (hippocampus) that explicitly remembers, which creates a gap between what the body knows (i.e., implicit memory) and the mind can recall (i.e., explicit memory)[27]. Gaps between the body's knowing and the mind's memory are like cracks in our bell. They deaden our resonance. And, just like the bell, we become both less sensitive to the energy around us (harder to get vibrating) and we can't amplify much of a signal (no ring).

Short of pathological extremes, many of us struggle with gaps between our implicit and explicit memories arising from our earliest relationships. As infants, we're totally dependent on attuned communication with an attentive, stable adult to get our needs met. About half of us are fortunate enough to have one such person in our life with whom we can establish this interpersonal resonance, leading to secure attachment. The other half are not so lucky, and will later struggle with unconscious behaviors manifesting anxiety, avoidance, disorganization or dissociation[28]. The unlucky half will be more likely, later in life, to manifest stress disorders (including PTSD) and be the kind of parents who resonate an insecure attachment with their children. And the beat goes on. As Dan Siegel points out, these effects arise through *relationship*, literally how we vibrate with another human being. "When the mind is doing well," Siegel concludes, "there is flow and harmony. When it's not doing well, there's rigidity and chaos."[29] As resonators, we not only subjectively experience our condition of harmony versus chaos; we export it. We also import the conditions of those we're close to.

Another consequence of our early-life relationships stems from how we try to get our needs met. From basic physical needs for food and warmth, to being safe, loved, respected and eventually, self-actualized, we have a whole Maslow's hierarchy of needs. We learn pretty early on that life isn't always going to meet them as we would like. For example, as we become socialized into our family, we might get our needs for safety, love and respect met by being the good kid who meets the expectations of others. We learn that when we do what's expected, we get safe, loving signals in return, which feels good—so we do it again. If we express unwelcome emotions or behaviors, we get clear signals to stop. At some point, it becomes clear that the only way to consistently get the warm, loving signals we desire is to pretend "good kid" on the outside, no matter what's going on inside. This is another kind of split that dulls our resonance and, perhaps later in life, we'll struggle with feeling like an imposter.

Or, say we decide to heck with being the good kid, if we can't get our needs met that way, and we'll substitute another need and settle for getting any kind of attention. What Arthur Janov observed is that, unlike natural needs for food, safety, love and so on, these substituted needs have no natural fill line[30]. So what we set up in this case is a loop in our system of resonance that is never satisfied—an unfillable hole. This distorts how we resonate by having to constantly feed itself. It becomes the point in why we do things—e.g., needing to be the center of attention. It throws us off from being able to naturally flow with the Way of things, where "in non-action we do everything." Forget that! Look at me!

Net net: it's easy for us to get stuck in habits that formed before we had much choice in the matter. It is also true that we can heal and re-establish the flow and harmony that is our mind and body resonating at its best.

GETTING IN SYNC

Healing from trauma, freeing up stuck points, particularly in the lower body, re-establishes a healthy flow of upward energy called, in yogic traditions, the liberating current. It's an essential contributor to the field we radiate and how we resonate. Similar to inhale and exhale, it pairs with the downward manifesting current to create a vital flow through our being, except instead of moving air, these currents move energy. The Western view finds a correlate to this energetic flow in the upward movement of electrically-charged, cerebral-spinal fluid. Regular breathing creates a slight oscillation in the spine that gently moves this fluid upward. Deep breathing regulated by muscles in the lower abdomen (i.e., *hara* breathing, which you'll have a chance to experience in Part II) supercharges this process, which generates a stronger electromagnetic field around the body.

Another sense of getting in sync comes from looking at brainwaves. The firing patterns of different regions of the brain have been well-studied using strap-on EEG caps whose many electrodes measure different brain regions simultaneously. Figure 2-3 summarizes the different brainwaves detected under different conditions. As brainwaves slow down, they more readily come into coherence across different regions of the brain, as well as with the heart. This adding up of signals is thought to be the foundation of subjective consciousness. As Tam Hunt puts it, macro-consciousness results "from a shared resonance among many micro-conscious constituents."[31]

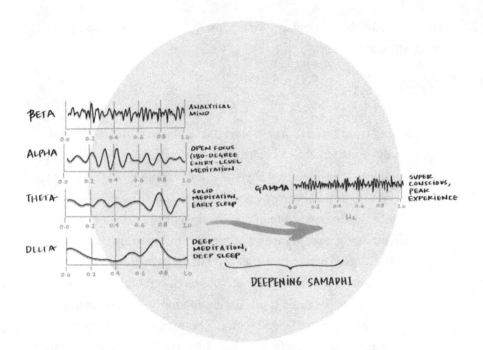

Figure 2-3. Your brain on meditation, sleep or peak experiences

Everyday, analytical mind is characterized by beta waves around 15-30 Hz. As the brain slows down in meditation or sleep, coherent alpha waves are created. As sleep or meditation deepens, waves slow down even further into the theta and delta range. From a state of deep, slow coherence, a super-conscious state can emerge, characterized by high-frequency gamma waves (50 Hz)[32]

Normal brain activity, what we experience as thinking about something using everyday analytical mind, registers as a fairly noisy set of signals around 30 Hz, called beta waves (Top line in Figure 2-3). Waves from different regions are each doing their own thing and don't add up; i.e., they're incoherent. They're like our little patch of Round Bay in Chapter 1, with many boats going back and forth, creating chop in the water.

When we shift to a more open focus, dropping into a more meditative, expansive state, the brain shifts into a slower, lower frequency and waves from different regions start adding up, creating coherent alpha waves in the range of 8–14 Hz (second line in Figure 2-3). In this state, more parts of the brain are communicating with one another and the overall effect is a clearer signal, an expanded state of consciousness. Little wonder that the expansive state of meditation proves to be more effective for inspiration than does staring at the problem.

Brain waves slow down further as we enter deeper states of meditation or sleep. Theta waves (4–8 Hz) characterize solid meditation and entry-level sleep (and meditators sometimes struggle with the boundary between the two). Even slower, more stable delta waves (.5–4 Hz) emerge in deep meditation and deep sleep, with clear, high amplitude signals being processed and generated. At slower alpha, theta and delta frequencies, brainwaves and heartbeats can synchronize (since hearts beat in this same range), leading to even more amplification. EEG studies have shown that the brainwaves of seasoned meditators show greater coherence not only in deep meditation, but also in daily activities, which matches the greater wholeness typically experienced by the meditators in their daily lives.[33] Indeed, the practices we'll introduce in Part II are designed to create a condition of complete awareness and complete relaxation at the same time, enabling us bring this stronger coherence into daily activities.

Finally, high-frequency, yet still highly coherent, gamma waves (>50Hz) indicate a state of super consciousness (right side of Figure 2-3). This expansive consciousness results from expanded resonance, as Hunt observes, "The shared resonance in a human brain that achieves gamma synchrony . . . includes a far larger number of neurons and neuronal connections than is the case for beta or theta rhythms alone.[34]" This isn't a state one could maintain indefinitely, but it corresponds to what people report as a peak experience. If Edgar Mitchell had been wearing an EEG device coming back from the moon, he probably would have registered gamma waves while his molecules were expanding across the universe. From a resonance point of view, it is a signal so powerful as to be life-changing.

Getting mind and body in sync not only feels good on the inside, it also sends a stronger, more coherent signal into the world. The lesson for resonance is that slowing down supports greater coherence (even the high-frequency gamma waves are only reached through the slower, coherent states), both within the brain and between brain and heart. While measurements that include the *hara* are just getting underway, my experience in martial arts would suggest even greater power and amplification is possible when head, heart and *hara* align. If the heart is an amplifier of the coherent brain, the *hara* is the powerful sub-woofer that adds organized movement, as we'll see in the energy patterns. The resonance of us-as-a-whole-person, clear as a bell, is a very different signal than what we transmit when we're stuck in old issues, stressed out, or jumping all over the place. Fortunately, we have support in generating system-wide resonance in the mind-body, given four energy patterns we can engage physically, conferring agility in how we handle and direct energy and well-being in our subjective experience. Let's move into them.

RESONATING IN FOUR PATTERNS

Josephine Rathbone was a keen observer. Working in the 1930s, she recognized four basic ways in which people moved and held residual tension in their bodies. At one extreme, people were tightly focused and at the other extreme, loosely put together. In between were two states where postures were properly held or rhythmically moving. In the 1960s, when electrophysiological measurements were possible, Valerie Hunt picked up Rathbone's work and found these four patterns corresponded to different orders in which nerves activated muscles. While Rathbone and Hunt speculated upon the connection to personality, it wasn't until choreographer Betsy Wetzig learned of this research that this connection was fully recognized. Betsy saw that these patterns explained so much about the differing traits of her dancers. For example, those who were excellent at the aggressive, thrusting moves of modern dance were also aggressive with her, and those who excelled in the precise *pliés* of ballet came to rehearsal on time and with clean outfits.

Betsy started connecting the dots between the physicality of the patterns and their emotional, cognitive and behavioral correlates. And when I met Betsy in 1998, she shared this treasure trove of insight with me, which led to our book, *Move to Greatness*[35]. It also led to decades of research into the patterns and to the FEBI°—the first personality assessment to link mind, body and behaviors[36]. Much has been written about the patterns elsewhere, but to summarize briefly: We now know that Rathbone's four movement patterns strongly correlate with the four dominant factors of personality. We know that when one part of the body enters a pattern, the rest of the body tends to follow, and that movement alone induces specific, subjective states (i.e., thoughts and emotions). We know that people have access to all four patterns, and also have pattern preferences that in some people are strong and in others, slight. And we know that the repetition of practice makes it easier to access any pattern one wants to cultivate.

So how do these four patterns resonate differently through our mind and body? From their names, you can get a feel for the quality of energy they bring to life: Driver pushes, Organizer holds form, Collaborator engages with rhythm, and Visionary expands into possibility. Through simple movements (see *Entering the Patterns*), you can experience each of these patterns and feel your own truth about their system-wide effects. Some commonly reported characteristics follow and are summarized in Table 2-1.

The pushy Driver sharply focuses energy to hit a target, push across the finish line, or beat a competitor. Driver energy is laser-focused on its intentions, rather than listening for new inputs. It gives rise to a subjective experience of fierce determination, sense of urgency, and often aggression. Its system-wide strength is in cutting out distractions and putting everything we've got behind a goal. Its weakness is that it may not be resonating with its environment, picking up important news and, as a result, it may have the wrong goal.

The Organizer turns energy into form. It takes in the energy of chaos and attempts to make order. It figures things out, step by step, to arrive at correct answers and proper actions. It gives rise to a subjective experience of calm discipline, logical thoughts, and conscientiousness. Its system-wide strength is to self-organize everything from our inner thoughts to our outward life into sensible compartments and reliable processes. Its weakness is that once those are established, it may not want to give them up, and ends up resonating with the past, not the present.

The rhythmic Collaborator plays in the to and fro of energy and can easily build resonance with other people. It dances with the energy around it, finding its way around obstacles, and playing in the give-and-take of dialogue. The subjective experience arising in this pattern has generally positive emotions, weighs multiple points of view, and rolls with the punches. Its system-wide strength is its contagious, positive outlook and personal resilience. Its weakness is that it may resonate with more than it can digest into action, and slosh from one dance to another.

Finally, the expansive Visionary rounds out this quartet with a big antenna for sensing energy and turning it into imagination and ideas. It leaps into the possibilities of futures not yet realized and problems not yet solved. Its subjective experience is frequently one of awe, inspired by nature, and freedom to explore. Its system-wide strength is its receptivity and imagination, which is able to leapfrog over constraining conditions. Its weakness is often being unable to turn its imagination into action or being misunderstood by others.

ENTERING THE PATTERNS

- **Push into Driver:** Stand up and press your big toes into the floor; push your hands together. Extend your arms straight out in front of you, palms pressed together and index fingers pointed. Site down your arms and index fingers as you continue pressing your hands and feet. If you can take several steps forward, do so quickly, and check your state.

(cont.)

- **Step into Organizer:** Stand still, perfectly balanced, as if a book were balanced on your head. Using your hands, mark the front, back, and sides of a box in the space in front of you where you wouldn't want a stranger standing. Take a step forward into this space and draw up your back foot. Step back and draw in your front foot. Step left and draw up. Step right and draw up. Repeat a few times until you feel what this pattern offers.

- **Swing into Collaborator:** Shift your weight from foot to foot, rocking your hips, and letting your whole body get rubbery. Bring your hands into the act, making an oscillating figure-8 or infinity symbol. Let the oscillations get larger and feel your whole body enter the easy, sloshing rhythm of this pattern. Notice any shift in mood.

- **Expand into Visionary:** Let your hands drift to the sides of your head, seeing both hands in your peripheral, 180-degree vision. Run the finger of your left hand along the underside of your right arm, and out through the backs of your fingertips, feeling this line of energy endlessly extending. Feel the same line of energy running through the left arm and out through its fingertips. Extending like a huge satellite dish, with the ease of a willow in the wind, expand into this pattern.

When these patterns play as a skillful quartet, our system-wide resonance is optimized for both sensing and action. The weaknesses of one pattern are mitigated by the strengths of another. Indeed, you can imagine the wide-ranging Visionary collecting inspiration that the Collaborator translates into dialogue, getting people moving with us. In comes the Organizer to put a process to our collective actions, and the Driver pushes our goal across the finish line. Feeling into the patterns in this order (which you can do by entering the patterns in a bottom-up series from Visionary to Driver), the body feels something like a bellows, taking in big energy and compressing it into a focused stream of activity—i.e., our very own Universal Energy Concentrator.

We can also look at these patterns from a chakra point of view, as each pattern is organized from a physical center that also maps to a specific chakra. In this view, the manifesting current of inspiring, Visionary energy (seventh chakra) descends through the body to be given form by the Organizer (third Chakra), engage others with the Collaborator (second chakra) and get it done with the Driver (first chakra). Likewise, the Driver is liberated from its blindness, the Collaborator from running in circles, and the Organizer from the past, through the upward liberating current, inspired by the Visionary in sympathetic vibration with universal energy.

Table 2-1. Characteristics of the Four Energy Patterns

	DRIVER	ORGANIZER	COLLABORATOR	VISIONARY
Movement, Physical Center	Push, thrust Base of abdomen, first chakra	Hold form, step Solar plexus, third chakra	Swing, rhythm Abdomen, second chakra	Expand, drift Top of head seventh chakra
Emotions and Thoughts	Intense, aggressive, sense of urgency, sharp, competitive, direct	Calm, stable, quiet, conscientious, proper, methodical, steady, process-oriented	Fun-loving, bright, cheerful, enthusiastic, engaging, people-person	Dreamy, open, expansive, outside of the box, imaginative, non-linear
Strength	Clarity, focus, cutting out distractions, intensely directs energy toward a target	Reliability, consistency, breaks big problems into steps, gives form to ideas	Resilience, rolling with punches, engaging people, finding a way around obstacles	Senses the big picture, gets at essence, opens to possibilities, lets go, curiosity
Weakness	Insensitive; could have wrong target	Attached to form, could get stuck in past	Running in circles, could lack direction, over-commit	Drifting off, fail to manifest vision, goal

Not only do these energies inspire and activate us as individuals, but also the people around us. As we resonate a stronger, clearer signal, it resounds through every relationship we're party to, just as those relationships form part of the universal energy that resounds through us.

SOCIAL RESONANCE

Given the importance of relationships to our life—we wouldn't be here without them—it's not surprising that the nervous system evolved "social circuitry," i.e., neurons and neural pathways that resonate with signals from other people and get them resonating with us. For example, if I see you smile, mirror neurons in me will start resonating to make a smile form on my lips. If I see you pick up a cup, a part of me is primed to pick up a cup. If I watch you win a gold medal in the Olympics, a part of me shares in that thrilling victory.

This internal resonance with other people is how we figure out what they're up to, and how we need to respond. Once we have a framework for sensing energy patterns, for example, we can feel in our own body what pattern someone is manifesting. We build internal maps of others by subtly mimicking their facial expressions and gestures, which gives us a subjective read on their emotions. In other words, we vibrate with them, largely unaware that we're doing it. As Guy Claxton writes, "[O]ur bodies are in a state of continual resonance with those around us—or those we may be remembering or imagining . . . While you and think we are discussing the film we've just seen, our bodies are dancing with each other's every gesture and expression."[37] What's more, this dance is essential to good communication. A study at Princeton University put two people in separate MRI neuroimaging machines and had one relay a story to the other. What they could see was the listener's brain mirroring the speaker's brain activity and, in some cases, jumping a bit ahead to anticipate where the story was going next. The stronger the match in signals between the two brains, the better the listener's understanding. And if the two brains don't get in sync, communication breaks down.[38]

While we tend to think of communication as passive listening and active speaking, resonance is bi-directional, and it's either happening or it's not. If we're not sensing or reading a person correctly, we're not on the same wavelength and our message is not going to resonate. When we sense something, we are literally vibrating with it, which means we are being changed by it. And if we're not willing to be changed, if we're resisting or blocking out what somebody is saying to us (which happens all the time in political conversations), we may hear the words, but we don't resonate with them. They're like a cosmic ray and our bell—zipping right by. What this means is that our ability to sense is what *enables* our ability to direct energy, affect other people, or make a difference. This gives us an important insight into how we apply resonance: if we want to make an even greater difference, we do well to explore how we can build even greater sensitivity.

When we do get on the same wavelength with people, our effects on them can be profound and beyond what we're even aware of. Joe Dispenza makes a powerful demonstration of this in his workshops, where he has people in the back of a large auditorium direct positive thoughts and emotions toward people sitting in the front row. The front row people, fitted with EEG caps, show greater brainwave coherence and synchronization at the very moment the positive thoughts start flowing[39]. Useful to remember in the many relationships of our life, that our positive intentions can be of service to people even before we open our mouths.

Through the relationships of our life, we become part of teams and networks of social systems. At their best, the groups we're a part of make us more creative and adaptive individuals and, conversely, we contribute to greater, transpersonal order through the groups we're a part of. You and I make a more effective and adaptive "we" when we're not only linked in communication, but able to harmonize our differing skills and gifts, something we'll apply to teams in Part III.

Dan Siegel demonstrates how this higher-level, self-organization comes about by bringing ten people who are reasonably comfortable singers up on stage during his talks. He first asks them to all sing the same note—a case of no differentiation. The result is an uninteresting monotone. He then asks them to plug their ears and each sing their own song. The result is chaos. Finally, he asks them to unplug their ears and sing a song they all know, e.g., "Amazing Grace." Each person brings a different voice, with self-organized, soaring harmonies that send chills through the audience.[40]

In addition to showing the conditions for social resonance, Siegel's demonstration shows how integration leads to higher levels of self-organizing complexity—i.e., exactly what Ilya Prigogine studied as the evolutionary direction of living systems. In other words, our mind and body reach their most evolved state of well-being when they're in flow and harmony, inside and out. If we're disconnected from people or disconnected within ourselves, rigidity or chaos develops. A rigid, tight muscle doesn't vibrate the same way as a relaxed one; it's like a musician playing off-key. A breakdown in communication in our relationships creates chaos; it's like a musician with plugged ears. Well-being arises when the system is integrated: each musician playing a relaxed, natural part, and easily vibrating with others.

What this tells us about our own life and its impact is that we evolve to our highest order when we're internally integrated and relaxed and externally harmonizing with others. Moreover, the internal and external conditions are entwined—just as we saw with our broken bell. Both our sensitivity and the ability to send a signal are deadened by the same break. Conversely, the sense of flow, harmony and well-being are pretty good guides to what it feels like when we get it right.

MIND-BODY AS ONE

An apocryphal scene is recounted at the beginning of the Surangama Sutra in which Gautama Buddha is asking his nephew,

Ananda (a frequent foil in these stories), where his mind his. Ananda knows this is a trick question, but points to his head anyway, and Buddha thunders back (I'm paraphrasing here), "That's not your mind! That's a thief who's stolen your identity!" Buddha would have much preferred Edgar Mitchell's answer that his mind was spread out through every molecule of the universe. Or the way Zen Master Omori Sogen put it: "The true human body is the entire universe."

This is not just a poetic possibility; it's the paradox of being human. We are both particular and universal. Yes, our mind uses our particular body and set of relationships to create itself and its sense of the world. And yes, the body, like all parts of the universe, is both hidden and manifest, both energy and matter, eating energy to evolve its order and capable of resonating with universal energy. From the boundlessness of universal energy, we can manifest new forms. Healing what's stuck or broken, we liberate ourselves to take in new energy. Our universal capacity and particular embodiment and relationships come together in a mind-body-as-one, doing one thing: resonating with the universe in accordance with our nature. And to the extent that we liberate ourselves to enjoy flow, harmony and well-being, we evolve our order, manifest our purpose, and become a force of nature.

Which inspires our work in Part II.

RESONANCE RECAP—MIND AND BODY

- Life is a special kind of system that can metabolize energy to evolve its order; we are resonators through and through.
- Our mind and body function on differing time scales: from seconds (thoughts) to minutes (emotions) to days and weeks (behaviors).
- Habits can get us locked in the past; getting in the habit of re-examining habits helps us engage the present moment.
- Elevated emotions and embodied practices amplify and bring endurance to the mind's intentions.
- Slowing down and unlocking from analytical mind supports greater coherence internally and in the signal we send to the world.
- Trauma and stored tension deaden resonance, making us less sensitive and less able to re-sound an effect.
- To sense is to vibrate with; to make a greater difference we need greater sensitivity.
- Four nervous system patterns support us in concentrating system-wide energy from far-reaching sensitivity to intense focus.
- When we're on the same wavelength with another, we are both changed; when we're not on the same wavelength, communication breaks down.
- We evolve to our fullest expression in flow and harmony, inside and out.

PART II

BECOME
A MORE
RESONANT
BEING

In which you learn practical ways to tune into universal
energy using the mind-body-as-one

3

INTEGRATE

It began with a self-defense class in college, my journey into martial arts. Initially, I just wanted to learn how to protect myself. But it was my passion for energy coupled with a world-class teacher, Toyoda Sensei, that deepened my decades-long dive into Aikido. Aikido, which literally translates as the Way (Do) to harmonize (Ai) energy (Ki), is ostensibly about using the energy of an attacker to take the person off balance into a throw or pin. But the deeper training of Aikido is how to harmonize with universal energy. Toyoda Sensei, who also trained in Zen, further led me to his teacher, the remarkable Tanouye Roshi.

Now something you should know about Tanouye Roshi is that his own Zen teacher said of him, "He's the kind of teacher who comes along once every 500 years." He was extraordinary in every way: if something valuable could be done by a human being, he would train himself to do it. By the time he was forty years old, he had attained a seventh degree black belt in four different martial arts (just for reference, I managed a fifth degree black belt in one martial art). He was also a music teacher and master of resonance. Resonance was our topic of conversation one evening, Tanouye Roshi and myself, sitting in the kitchen of the dojo in Hawaii. I don't recall exactly what I was mid-sentence saying with all my physics and words, but Tanouye's face took on a wry expression and, quite suddenly, the lights blinked. "Did you do that!?" shot out of my mouth, but he'd already made his point. OK, two learnings: I didn't know squat, and never underestimate what's possible for a fully integrated human being. Now perhaps blinking the lights is not quite the difference you want to make. But the amount of energy he could concentrate into that moment was not unlike what he put into his teaching, which is why his teaching penetrated to my bones. It's also why I continue to be guided by him daily, though he died sixteen years ago. And I'm not alone. Dozens of his students could tell similar stories. He made a difference—one could argue he's still making it— that transcends life and death.

How can each of us make a difference that is both true to us and true in a larger sense—aligned with the Way? We start inside out, integrating our mind-body-as-one, that we can tap into the resourcefulness of the universe played through our particular life in our particular context. Although I use words to point to it, the answer lies not in words, but in practice. For the key is to unlock this material body so that it vibrates with a broader range of universal energy, and the mind emerging from this clear-sensing, relational body can direct that energy into actions with less resistance and greater clarity. As Chapter 2 made clear, we can't just skip the body and work mindfully, much as the ego may want us to think so. The ego can play many games with our thoughts, but the body does not lie, and neither does it belie the past it grew up through. Integrating our whole instrument is the way to getting energy flowing without obstruction, which both liberates the past and manifests the future ready to happen through our present being. To support us in this work is a Zen toolkit of integrative practices leveraging:

- One Breath,
- Two Sides—yin and yang,
- Three Centers—head, heart and *hara*,
- Four Energy Patterns—Driver, Organizer, Collaborator and Visionary.

Armed with this toolkit, we'll pull together those metaphorical pieces rolling around in the bottom of the ACME box, so that we can use our fully integrated mind-body-as-one. Let's start with something you already have and are never without: breath, supported by *hara*.

ONE BREATH

Dennis is a kind man. A skillful facilitator of leadership development, Dennis has a background in Gestalt psychology and a keen ability to catch himself in his own tricks. "At times, I've found myself rescuing a dysfunctional team because I'm uncomfortable with their conflict," he admits. "I would beat myself up if a session didn't go well, because I thought my job was to make everything right." Several years ago, Dennis asked me to show him how to meditate, and he picked up the practice. He was among the first to attend leadership programs at IZL, and eventually decided to throw himself into the intensive training of *sesshin*. No spring chicken, he found the training exhausting, and on his drive home he felt like an utter failure who had wasted his time. Waking up the next morning, he discovered what's on the other side of exhausting the self. "During *sesshin*, I became much more disciplined about exhaling slowly and as long as I could, and I could experience my *hara* more viscerally. Now, I can go to that centered place anytime I'm feeling small or stuck. I can face my fears from a bigger perspective, which reduces them to annoying—not overwhelming. I can bring stillness to myself in a new way. I'm also more sensitive to the breathing rhythms and body cues of others, and can pick up on their moods more quickly. I feel more alive."

What Dennis learned to do—slowing down his breathing using the *hara*—changed how he resonated internally and changed what others sensed from him. His colleagues started describing him as more grounded, courageous, and calm. It changed his felt sense of connectedness and aliveness, made him better able to sense the wavelength of others and get on it. It also changed how he worked:

"For the first time, I had the experience of a larger force working through me rather than me trying to make something happen. In my work, I no longer go into 'fix it' mode or try to finesse a meeting or rescue a team. I challenge them authentically and with compassion. The qualitative difference in my relationships is I can resonate with what wants to happen in that moment rather than trying to manifest a made-up reality. I am literally living life, at least to the fullest I am capable of now."

Dennis is a humble man—in fact, I'm sure he'd want me to quit talking about him right now—and he'd be quick to point out that he might still have this flaw or that fault. But here's what's wonderful: we don't have to be flawless or fault-free to make a difference or have a "larger force" coming through us. Limitless energy can work through a limited self when we vibrate more freely with it. Dennis' approach, starting with breath, is a perfect way to open up our Zen toolkit and start using its richness. If we think of Zen as a technology for integrating the whole Self, breath is the first "app." We'll put it at the pinnacle of our toolbox (see Figure 3-1) and add to it throughout the chapter. But first, a few things you should know about breath:

Figure 3-1. Integration Starts with One Breath

Breath is a bridge. The rate at which we breathe is one of the fundamental vibrations in the human body, and is tied to other rhythms, such as our heart rate and the rate at which our mind chatters. So it's not surprising that how we breathe has a great deal to do with how we resonate. Unlike these other rates, our respiratory rate is consciously controllable. Yet, when we're not conscious of breathing, we're still breathing, which tells us that breath is a unique bridge between conscious and unconscious mind and body. For that reason, every form of meditation and for that matter, excellence in any sport, martial art, or way of using the body will emphasize breathing. When we integrate our One Breath into what we do, we do it better.

Slower is better. Slowing our breath rate drops us into a lower, slower frequency, which can be heard in our voice, seen in our actions, and resonates to others as calm confidence. Conversely, when we're hyperventilating or panting, our breath comes high and fast in the chest, and our voice sounds anxious and edgy. A lower, slower rate of breathing also allows for greater coherence between heart and head. It creates a condition of relaxed, flowing energy and greater sensitivity to what is going on. Just as we saw on Round Bay in Chapter 1, big, slow waves can hold and entrain faster ripples, but not the other way around. So slower is a better container for coherence—both internally and with other people. We could liken our inner state to waves on water. At a low, slow frequency, the waves are few and far between, and the "vibe" of other people and the outer world is more clearly reflected in the water. With high frequency chop, the agitated water distorts everything reflected in it. And so it is with us.

Deeper is better. Related to our rate of breathing is the depth from which the breath is drawn and to which it penetrates. The lungs are not able to move under their own power, so they need muscles to help them, and the job is done more or less completely depending on which muscles are doing the work. If the muscles high in our chest are given the job, only the top of the lungs fill and to get enough oxygen to run our whole system, they have to work quickly. Moreover, we lose the lung capacity we don't use, and the stale air in our lower lung becomes acidic. When the diaphragm muscle is given the job, it's able to pull breath more deeply into the lungs, but still not all the way down. When muscles deep in the lower abdomen—i.e., the *hara*—are regulating the breath, they suck it to the very depth of the lungs and expel it completely. *Hara* breathing is the slowest, deepest, most efficient breath our bodies are capable of. Since we have to breathe anyway, why not do it right?

Here's a practice you can do anytime, anyplace: deepen your inhale and lengthen your exhale. Deepening your inhale means expanding muscles as far down in the abdomen as you can access to take in a breath. Lengthening your exhale means letting your breath out slowly through your nose, as if it were on a gravity feed dropping down through your body, through your *hara*, through your feet into the earth. Most people breathe in and out about ten times a minute. Slow that down to two or three times a minute and your entire condition changes, as well as what you resonate to others, as Dennis discovered.

By generating a big, slow wave of deep breathing, you create a foundation for integrating your whole system. If you want to get better at this, I invite you to immerse yourself into the *One Breath* exercise (see box). A video of this exercise, along with others in this book, is available at https://resonatethebook.com. I box up the exercises and put many of them on the website so you can skip over them now and come back to them later if you just want to keep on reading. But I include them because resonance springs to life through experience, not concepts, and I'd wish for you to experience resonance as deeply as possible. As for this breathing exercise, I do it every morning.

In addition to slowing down your breath, another integrating practice that bears wonderful fruit is to do everyday activities one-with breath. The exhale is the relaxing part of the breath cycle. When timed with fast moves, it makes us more powerful and, when timed with slow moves, it lets us be more sensitive and calm. In either case, integrating our exhale with our actions lets us resonate more coherently. If you're doing something exacting, like threading a needle, start exhaling and then perform your exacting motion. (Try this with a real needle and thread and notice the difference in ease between threading it on an exhale versus on an inhale). If you need to push a heavy object, take in a breath, set your *hara* and start your push on the exhale. If you're cutting vegetables, start on an exhale and feel the exhale flowing through subsequent cuts. As I write, I find that a long exhale helps the words flow out more evenly. Discover the countless ways that working with One Breath can support you.

IMMERSION INTO ONE BREATH

- **Set the *hara*.** Stand comfortably, feet shoulder width, knees soft, weight on the balls of your feet. Let your eyes soften, that you can see all around you (180-degree vision) and nothing in particular. Press your hands together and press your big toes into the earth and notice a "thereness" or muscular alertness at the base of your abdomen as you start pressing. "Setting the hara" is activating this base. Try this a few times, sending your exhale down through this base with as little pressure as possible while still feeling the *hara* set (see Figure 3-2a).

- **Expand the belly.** Now imagine your belly as an expandable balloon. Place your hands on your lower abdomen and breathe slowly in and out through your nose, letting tension drop away with every exhale until you can feel your breath move under your hands. (see Figure 3-2b). Notice if you set the *hara* on the exhale that the belly does not deflate or lose its sense of expansion.

- **Inhale #1.** Relax on the inhale and let your hands rise to your solar plexus, palms up, allowing the breath to fill the belly from the bottom (see Figure 3-2c).

(cont.)

- **Exhale #1**. As you begin your exhale, turn your palms to the ground and gently push them down, setting your *hara* by directing your breath straight down through the base of the *hara*, and down through the balls of your feet. Let your *hara* stay expanded (see Figure 3-2d).

- **Inhale #2**. Relax on the inhale and let your hands rise overhead, extending upward (see Figure 3-2e).

- **Exhale #2**. As you begin your exhale, set your *hara*, extend big toes into the earth, and let your arms arc slowly back to center, keeping your eyes 180 degrees and seeing both hands in your peripheral vision. Keep an expansive, big feeling throughout the exhale and in the *hara* (Figure 3-2f). Release and relax on the inhale as your hands rise up and the in-breath comes to you (Figure 3-2c). Continue alternating the two patterns for several minutes.

Table 3-2. Deep, slow *hara* breathing

TWO SIDES

"I used to try to control 'out there,'" Glynnis answered when I caught up with her about a year after she'd come through her first *Zen Leader* program. You might remember Glynnis from the Introduction, as she has inspired further work—including this book—on how Zen and Zen leadership can help us address big, hairy issues like climate change. She is deeply committed to making a better, more sustainable world, but on this day, we were talking about how the tools of Zen had helped her personally and in running her company. "Now I feel more connected, less needing to force things. You can ask anyone here, there's been a real shift. We'd always get the work done," she went on, "but it used to make me tired and irritable. I felt I had to impose myself on others—force things to happen. Now I feel this expansiveness—a broader consciousness—and I let people make their contributions respectfully. I work less because others work more and well."

Listening to Glynnis, I could imagine being one of her employees and how different it would feel to be controlled vs. connected. In resonating with others, we play in the paradox of self and other, engaging in the give-and-take of relationship where, at best, we each contribute our best, and build off the other's energy, creating something greater than either of us alone. Glynnis' experience leads us into the next tier of our Zen toolkit, namely how to make the best of Two Sides.

What do we know about paradox and managing Two Sides well?

Everything has Two Sides. Carl Jung once observed that paradox comes closest to accurately describing reality. For as soon as we define a term, we imply its opposite—like the peak and trough of a wave, there's no peak without a trough. Yin implies yang. Self implies other. In practical terms, we're faced with paradoxical choices every day, for example, between how much we try to control vs. connect, focus on self vs. others, tasks vs. people, short term vs. long term, cost vs. quality, work vs. family and on and on. Building off the work

Figure 3-3. Embracing two sides

of Barry Johnson[41], one of the "flips" I write about in *The Zen Leader* is to go from "or" to "and" thinking, recognizing that tending to only one side eventually lands us in a heap of trouble[42]. Instead, we do well to see Two Sides, understand the up- and downsides of each (i.e., Map 4), and develop measures or signals to know when to shift focus from one side to the other (e.g., Manage the Figure-8). The exercise—*Stepping into Two Sides*—is a variant on this process.

Two Sides imply dynamism. If you shift to and fro, making a figure-8 with your hands (as we did in experiencing Collaborator energy in the previous chapter), you can feel that the movement between Two Sides has a rhythm—i.e., a vibrational frequency. For example, moving between the two sides of inhale and exhale, our frequency might be several times a minute. For shifting focus between work and family, our frequency might be much slower, maybe twice a day. The dynamism between Two Sides is movement between what is manifest (e.g., our focus, current activity) and what is hidden. We could say when we're manifesting inhale, exhale is hidden, and when we're manifesting exhale, inhale is hidden. But as the yin-yang symbol reminds us, the hidden is *in* the manifest and the manifest is *in* the hidden and one is forever becoming the other. The point is, nothing exists statically because everything is in dynamic movement, again like the peaks and troughs of a wave where we see the peaks, but not the troughs. Know that the troughs are there, even when you don't see them. Know that what you see is always rising or falling, even when it seems immovable.

Two sides point to a greater truth. One of the steps in managing paradox is to articulate the higher-level goal or truth that comes about through the best of both sides. For example, as Glynnis manages the paradox of controlling her company and connecting with her employees, the higher level goal might be a connected control that resonates with the market and with her people. Moreover, the dynamic movement between Two Sides builds energy—i.e., resonance. When we use Two Sides to point to a greater truth, we unlock from habitual thinking and open into a more expansive condition where new inputs can change us. We open ourselves to more energies, and the higher-level goodness that can arise from Two Sides.

Working with Two Sides is a key tool for our integration as it points us toward a way to resolve dualistic thinking and unlock from one-sided views. Ultimately, it lets us grapple with the paradox of being human: a universal Self expressed through a particular body. A whole Self whose "true human body is the entire universe" and a local self who has to meet deadlines and pick up the kids. A manifesting presence of universal energy, and an animal with a fierce instinct to survive. All are true, but our particular, local, living and dying self is mostly manifest, while the whole Self is largely hidden, albeit in plain sight.

Here is a practice you can do anytime, with any person: become the other. If I am the other person, how would I be with them? If that other person is, in a sense, a hidden part of me, how do I lift them up, learn from them? If that person irritates me or I feel resistance to becoming them, what are they showing me about myself that is normally hidden? Start by simply getting curious about the other's reality, how they look

STEPPING INTO TWO SIDES

- **Select a topic and a person.** Start by picking an important matter in your life where you're wanting to make a difference, and pick a person ("X") who matters importantly in that. Using tape or sticks on the floor, make a "+" sign large enough that you could stand in any of its 4 quadrants. Likewise make a large "+" sign on a piece of paper so you can record your answers as you move through each quadrant. Label the "horizontal" axis with you on one end and person X on the other (as in Figure 3-4a). The upper two quadrants will represent what's good and valuable about what each side brings to this matter, and the lower quadrants will represent concerns if that side acted alone or that side has about the matter. You can make this a purely paper exercise if movement isn't possible, but you'll find it's more powerful when you physically move your body.

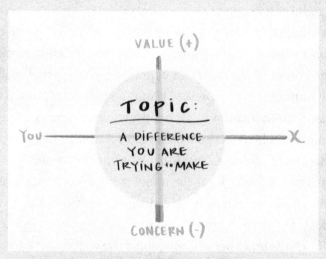

Figure 3-4a. Identifying Two Sides

(cont.)

- **Step into the upper left quadrant** and feel into what's good and valuable about your side, and what you're trying to do. Write down what's valuable and also what you feel standing here.

- **Move down into the lower left quadrant** and feel into your concerns about this matter, especially if you act in isolation. Notice what it feels like in your body to be standing in this quadrant, and jot down the issues, emotions and sensations you perceive here.

- **Step across to the upper right quadrant** and become person X. Feel into what you-as-X find good or valuable in this matter and what's valuable in you-as-X that this matter might bring out. Write down what value X can bring and how X feels when valued.

- **Move down into the lower right quadrant** and, still as X, feel into the concerns you-as-X have in this matter, and what it feels like to stand here. Write down what issues, emotions and sensations you have. You should now have entries in all four quadrants (i.e., Map 4, Figure 3-4b).

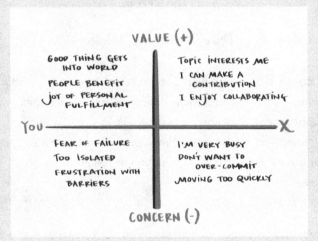

VALUE (+)

GOOD THING GETS INTO WORLD
PEOPLE BENEFIT
JOY OF PERSONAL FULFILLMENT

TOPIC INTERESTS ME
I CAN MAKE A CONTRIBUTION
I ENJOY COLLABORATING

You — X

FEAR OF FAILURE
TOO ISOLATED
FRUSTRATION WITH BARRIERS

I'M VERY BUSY
DON'T WANT TO OVER-COMMIT
MOVING TOO QUICKLY

CONCERN (-)

Figure 3-4b. Map Value and Concerns of Two Sides

(cont.)

- **Stand at the top** of your "+" sign, facing the quadrants, and open your palms as if to hold the Two Sides of you and person X all at once (Figure 3-4c). Feel into the bigness of being both of you, and what is true from that whole perspective. Take three slow hara breaths, feeling into X as part of you, you as part of X, both you and X as part of the Way, and let emerge any guidance or emotion from this expansive state.

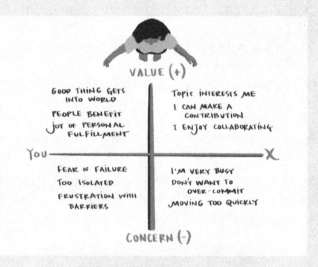

Figure 3-4c. Becoming Two Sides

- **Capture** any overarching goal or re-framing of the matter that comes from this expansive state, and any advice for how you approach it and best engage X. To the extent that you can connect this matter to what matters to X, mitigate X's concerns, and connect X to the bigness you're feeling now, you'll build resonance with X.

at the world, at an issue at hand, at you. Listen with every pore of your skin, suspending judgment in favor of simply sensing them. Know that everything you sense is helping you get on the same wavelength with them, should that be important. It's also bringing you one person closer to your whole Self—seeing the part of you that is not the usual suspect.

The exercise, *Stepping into Two Sides*, gives you a way to further play in Two Sides of self and other and the greater truth of resonating as the whole picture.

THREE CENTERS

Aimee teaches tenth grade, when she's not teaching Aikido or training in Zen. And she finds her training has helped her "sink down in the middle of crazy with a clear mind to act." Occasionally in her teaching, she encounters angry parents who are afraid for their underperforming children. One day, she was holding a three-way conference involving one such parent and a student who chronically skipped class and didn't do his homework. "Account for your actions," Aimee said to the student who had just missed class again. The mother jumped up, ready to walk out in a huff, angrily defending her son. Rather than get upset, Aimee distinctly felt herself sinking down into her *hara*. Awareness expanding further, she could see what was happening, and calmly respond to the mother, "I'm very sorry that's the impact I'm having. I care about this person." The fight drained out of the mother as she could feel their common caring for her son, and they were able to hold a productive meeting. Working with the Three Centers from the bottom up—*hara* centeredness first, followed by a heartfelt connection, and finally the head's discourse—Aimee was able to turn a confrontation into a resonant parent-teacher collaboration.

The bottom-up order in which Aimee successfully engaged her Three Centers was not a coincidence—it was how she trained in the dojo. And neither was the productive outcome likely any other way. If she had started with the head, lacking sensitivity and a heart connection, her words would not have resonated. Connecting with heart, she might have gotten on the same wavelength with the parent, but lacking the centeredness of *hara*, she could have been pulled off course and her words wouldn't have held such conviction. But building a foundation of strength from the base, she was able to steady the emotions of a heartfelt connection, making the head's communication more courageous and connected.

As we saw in Chapter 2, the Three Centers of head, heart and *hara* have physical correlates in terms of multiple brains and energetic correlates in the chakras. Representing, in a sense, the differing time scales of thoughts, feelings and actions, their integration increases our range of sensitivity to the energy around us and amplifies what we're able to do with it. Moreover, it brings us into a coherent whole, where our walk wholeheartedly matches our talk. We make these Three Centers the next tier in our toolkit for integrating mind-body-as-one to resonate at our best.

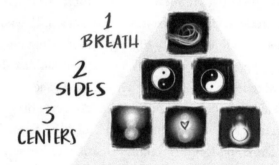

Figure 3-5. Integrating Three Centers

Let's review what each of these centers contributes to our integrated resonance.

Hara needs reclaiming. Owing to our bottom-up development, many people are cut off from their *hara* as part of embodying childhood habits, learning impulse control, stuffing tension, or holding trauma. The deep psoas muscles in this area are notorious among bodyworkers (and anyone who's had deep bodywork done) for holding tension, and deep bodywork is an excellent way to release it. Yoga, Pilates, martial arts, sports and even daily activities can be used to develop the *hara*. Table 3-1 lists several such activities with ways to put *hara* into them. My colleague, Ken Kushner Roshi, has a blog and bountiful resources for *hara* development at https://haradevelopment.org.

Hara is the gateway to Samadhi. Perhaps because this center developed before our sense of a separate self, it functions from an intrinsic sense of connectedness—a gut level knowing that is not intellectual, but more like sensing rhythms and moving with them. Like a surfer catching a wave, or a dancer moving to music, when we operate from the intuitive knowing of the *hara*, we simply move one-with. When we breathe deeply to and from this area, our breath slows down enough to invite the connected consciousness we call Samadhi. Moreover it feels good. Among the messaging from the gut to the brain are signals that calm us down, create a sense of well-being, and cut discursive thinking.

ACTIVITIES	FOCUS ON. . .
Martial arts, e.g., kendo, aikido, karate, tai chi, boxing, kickboxing	Dynamic movement from *hara* and powering body movements from *hara*
Kyudo (Japanese archery), archery	Coordinating breath, body movement, and *hara*
Zumba, Pilates, Yoga, ways of developing "core," many forms of dance	Moving from hara and, in some cases, breathing to *hara*
Swinging, striking sports: e.g., baseball, golf, bowling, tennis, racquetball	Keeping upper body relaxed and powering movement from *hara*
Lifting heavy objects, pushing heavy objects	Lifting or pushing from *hara*, coordinated with breath; keeping shoulders relaxed
Cutting motions, e.g., gardening, cooking, wood splitting	Setting the *hara*, working with breath, and making each cut clean
Walking	Moving from *hara* first, with a relaxed body along for the ride, breathing to and from hara

Table 3-1. Ways of Engaging and Developing *Hara*

Heart is an amplifier. If anything runs better with a sense of well-being, it's the heart. The heart simply functions better in the presence of positive emotions. And if anything amplifies our signal in the world or makes us more emotionally sensitive to others, it's the heart. When the *hara* is doing its job of maintaining a foundational connection, it supports a happier heart by allowing less room for fear to grow or negative emotions to take over. For heart to resonate optimally, it needs to feel relaxed and open, not tight and constricted. Yoga, in particular, offers postures and practices to help open the heart, as does the exercise, *Integrating the Three Centers* (see box).

Head has the greatest potential for wisdom and delusion. Our head brain with its sensory organs and pineal gland and 100 billion densely-woven nerve cells radically expands the energies we can vibrate with. At its best, it's our wide-open link to universal energy, and the thoughts it generates arise from the wisdom of connectedness—i.e., Samadhi. At its worst, it's ignoring much of present energy available, while it's lost in thought, imagination, neurotic loops, second guessing, doubts, fears and crap from the past. Even though our subjective experience of mind is derived from all Three Centers, as well as relational energy outside of the body, head-thoughts can steal the show. Moreover, head-thoughts are most prone to delusion, as they originate from a perspective that is blind to its own distortions. As physicist David Bohm put it, "The mind creates the world and then says, 'I didn't do it!'" Our head-thoughts would have us believe we're taking in the world just as it is. Never mind that the only way we pick up anything about the outside world is by vibrating with it, and what we're capable of vibrating with is limited by our sensors, attention biases, memory and learning.

Fortunately, we can expand our range, and have a richer experience of the world. But to do so, we have to divert more attention toward present-moment sensing and away from thought. Second, we can expand our attentional focus to nothing in particular, and create slower, more coherent brainwaves. Third, we can train the mind to develop a perspective on itself—i.e., a Witness perspective—where it begins to catch itself in its own tricks. Meditation is the oldest and most reliable practice for doing all three.

We'll come back to guidance for a meditation practice in Chapter 5, but here's a simple starting point for getting the head into a state where it can be readily integrated with heart and *hara*. We incorporate this practice into meditation, but you can use it in many other settings as well (maybe not while driving or reading this book!). Drop your gaze so that it splashes off the floor some distance in front of you, maybe six feet or a couple meters. Open your hands and, starting with your thumbs in your ears, extend your hands to either side, tracking them with peripheral vision only. Bring your hands slightly behind your head until you can just barely see them. Keeping this 180-degree vision, focus on nothing in particular and sense everything in general. This helps the brain disengage from beta waves and settle into more coherent alpha waves. Feel your breath move in your body, and your entire system settle down, like a pond on a calm day.

To take this further, make a practice of the exercise, *Integrating the Three Centers*, while standing, sitting, and lying down. By connecting head-thoughts to hara-breath, you close the loop among the Three Centers, allowing them to harmonize. You might make a practice of the lying-down version anytime you're upset or need to rest. You might do the sitting version when you need relaxed concentration. You might do the standing version when you need to summon your full strength for an important engagement.

INTEGRATING THE THREE CENTERS

Lying Down—This is easiest position for getting the feel for *hara* breathing because the body is most relaxed. To start, lie down in a place where your big toes can make contact with a vertical surface, e.g., a wall or a headboard.

(cont.)

a. **Expand and Engage *Hara*.** Place your hands on your *hara* and inhale deeply, feeling the *hara* expand under your hands. As you begin your exhale, gently extend your big toes into the vertical surface, setting the *hara*. Exhale slowly through your hara, down through your big toes. Exhale slowly through your *hara*, down through your big toes. Release and relax on the inhale, re-expanding the *hara*. Engage and extend big toes on the exhale. Maintain this rhythm throughout.

b. **Open and Settle Heart.** On an exhale, as you feel the breath dropping down through your body, imagine it carrying away any tension in your heart area. On an inhale, feel *hara* physically expand and imagine the heart energetically expanding (i.e., feel expansive without puffing up your chest). On the exhale, expand into the space around the heart, and let all tension drain down and out.

c. **Expand and Free Head.** Maintain 180-degree vision, and calmly attend to the movement of breath through the stabilizing *hara*, passing through and bringing peace to the head.

Sitting—Similar to lying down, but now you can make use of gravity. Sit in a way where your big toes can make contact with the floor.

a. **Expand and Engage *Hara*.** Feel the *hara* expand on an inhale. As you begin your exhale, gently extend your big toes into the earth, letting your breath simply drop down in gravity. Release and relax on the inhale, re-expanding the *hara*. Engage and extend big toes on the exhale. Maintain this rhythm throughout.

b. **Open and Settle Heart.** Same as for lying down, now adding the feel of gravity simply draining tension down and away from the heart, out through the feet.

(cont.)

c. **Expand and Free Head.** Same as for lying down, now adding the feel of how dropping breath down in the field of gravity also creates lift through the spine and top-back of the head.

Standing—6-Point Check: Same as above, now with your legs under you. Stand with soft knees, letting weight drop toward the front of your feet, toward the big toes. Do this 6-point check from the bottom up (see Figure 3-6):

1. Weight in big toes
2. Knees soft
3. Hara expanded and naturally weighted in gravity
4. Heart expanded into the space around it, shining straightforward, aligned in gravity
5. Eyes 180-degrees, focused on nothing in particular
6. Feel breath moving through the body, expanding hara on inhale, draining down in gravity

Figure 3-6. Point check

FOUR ENERGY PATTERNS

Beth is an accomplished physician who has trained in Zen and Zen leadership for several years. She also leads a department of healthcare practitioners and employee wellness at a major university, meaning she attends a lot of meetings. "I now think about the four energy patterns all the time at work," she said. "I'm always asking, 'OK, which pattern does this situation need: Driver, Organizer, Collaborator or Visionary? What's that person's general energy?'" She has learned to read cues for which energy pattern a person manifests in the moment. For example, if someone is leaning in and acting impatient, she picks up on their Driver energy. "If they're in Driver mode, I know to get to the point, but don't make it a contest of wills." She has learned to read the energy of a meeting. For example, when it's flat and rote with too much Organizer energy, she knows to brighten it up with some Collaborator engagement, having people share stories or discuss in pairs the people implications of a pending decision. "The patterns have really helped me, not only to read the situation around me, but also to see myself. And if I'm not in the right energy for what the situation calls for, I know how to shift."

Being in the right energy for the person or situation we face is a system-wide way we can match the specificity that resonance relies on. Remember, energy has to match for resonance to occur, and the energy patterns give us a simple way to keep shifting our frequency until we sense something catching on. As such we make the Four Energy Patterns the final tier in our Zen toolkit for integrating our self, both in an embodied way and in relationship to the world around us.

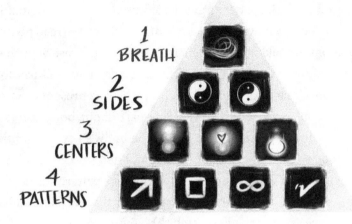

Figure 3-7. Resonating in Four Energy Patterns

Let's look at how we can make the patterns work to integrate inside and out.

Patterns enable agility. The Driver pushes and clarifies, the Organizer takes steps and holds form, the Collaborator rhythmically engages, while the Visionary expands and imagines. As we saw in Chapter 2, these four patterns work best as a harmonious quartet, even if one or two take the lead in our personality, which is generally the case. They complement one another's strengths and mitigate weaknesses. Once we know what our go-to patterns are (which is where the FEBI is useful), we can ask how we might approach a person or situation using one of our weaker, but still available, patterns. How would a Collaborator start this conversation? What would an Organizer do here? The simple movements in Chapter 2 gave you a feel for each pattern, and more ways of accessing and developing the patterns are listed in Table 3-2. The point is: being able to move freely from one pattern to another widens the range of people and situations we can resonate with. Conversely, if we fail to access a pattern when it's called for, we create a dead zone in our ability to resonate.

Patterns bring subtle cues to conscious awareness. As Beth experienced daily, the patterns give us a framework for recognizing what kind of energy is at play in people or situations. We read people and situations by making internal maps of them. In the case of people, we subtly mimic their gestures and facial expressions—all passing beneath conscious awareness—which creates a representation of them inside our own bodies. When one part of our body enters a pattern, it tends to spread to the rest of the body, so even a subtle, unconscious signal has a way of being amplified into a conscious, system-wide effect as we start to feel the other's pattern inside our self. In the case of situations, we get a feel for their rhythm: What kind of a wave are we trying to catch? The more we do this, as with honing any sense, the better we get at it.

Table 3-2. Practices to Develop Each Energy Pattern

	DRIVER	ORGANIZER	COLLABORATOR	VISIONARY
At Work	Know your top three priorities Measure something you're doing and cut it in half Get to the point Set stretch goals Reduce distractions Enforce clarity, action, and accountability	Make a list Organize your day Preserve time for planning Break big jobs down into steps Always know your next step Under-promise and over-deliver	Put fun into your day, celebrate Build your network Bond a team you're working with See both sides Find your way around obstacles; play in the give and take Work through people	Add spontaneity to your day Make time for reflection Brainstorm, ideate Widen your perspective (e.g., surf the net, solicit many points of view) Create some chaos, stir things up

	DRIVER	ORGANIZER	COLLABORATOR	VISIONARY
Supporting Activities Outside of Work	Running; activities done hard and fast Weightlifting Competitive sports Competitive martial arts Activities done sharply, with edge, pushing, or cutting movements	Walking; activities done step-by-step Activities done holding form, e.g., yoga, ballet, dressage, meditation Activities to create order, e.g., cleaning house, office or desk Activities that shape things: woodworking, needlepoint, ceramics Anything done to a process	Rocking; activities done with people and rhythm Dance (with partner) Aikido Social sports, especially with swinging movements, e.g., golf, bowling Team sports Funny games, improvisational comedy Playing with children or pets	Expanding; activities that explore and be Activities emphasizing energy or being in the moment, e.g, Tai Chi, Chi Kung, meditation (Samadhi) Activities done out in nature, e.g., hiking in mountains, sailing Activities with drifting movements, e.g., hang-gliding, scuba diving, snorkeling Aesthetic arts, Feng Shui
Sensory Support	Office: Stark and sparse furnishings Music: Rock & Roll, Rap; hit on the beat Art: Sharp, high contrast, sports posters, "Winning"	Office: Neat and tidy, a place for everything Music: Classical; place on the beat Art: Still life, perfectly composed, "Quality is . . ."	Office: fun and colorful, over-stuffed furnishings Music: Jazz; swing on the beat Art: family photos, comic strip characters, "Hang in there, Baby"	Office: light and airy, harmony with nature Music: New Age; hang on the beat, if there is one Art: Enigmatic, evocative, outer space posters, "Imagine . . ."

Adapted from: G. Whitelaw, The Zen Leader, pp 122-123.
Used with permission.

Patterns give us choice in how to direct energy. Once we read a person or situation, it doesn't mean we're confined to the same pattern in order to resonate. But it generally means that's a good place to start in order to join, and then go from there. To recount Beth's example when sensing someone in Driver, she knew she had to meet that energy with a clear point, but not just stay in Driver and thus make it a battle of wills. Or, in the meeting that had too much Organizer energy, she didn't want to keep adding Organizer to it. But she could make an Organizer move to bring out Collaborator energy by slotting a Collaborator activity into the agenda. Beyond reading and responding to the energy of people and situations, the patterns also give us choice in how much we direct our energy toward the far-reaching sensing and being of Visionary, as opposed to the intensely focused doing of Driver, with Collaborator and Organizer in between. Are we more antenna or arrow? A good rule of thumb is be an arrow when you know you've got the right target. Otherwise, be an antenna.

If you find that you're not able to integrate one or more of the energy patterns into your repertoire, Table 3-2 is for you. It suggests a number of practices that develop any pattern you'd like easier access to. Remember, "easier access" means you're laying down or strengthening specific pathways in your nervous system—itself an act of internal resonance that requires repetition. But the good news is: once the road is there, you can drive on it anytime. Once the pattern is strongly embodied, you don't have to think about it: it will function as needed. And you'll find life takes on a natural, sustainable balance when the nervous system can move freely in all Four Energy Patterns. You'll also find life will keep presenting challenges that will call for different energies at different times. Sometimes we have to push, sometimes hold, sometimes play well with others, and sometimes leap to what's next. We can either develop agility in the Four Energy Patterns, reclaim our full, natural energy, and resonate with what life presents—or miss opportunities and struggle. Those are pretty much the options.

By engaging the Four Energy Patterns, harmonizing the Three Centers, resolving the Two Sides, and letting One Breath flow through all that we do, we integrate our whole mind-body system into a more resonant instrument, more capable of both sensing and directing energy. How can we further tune this instrument to ring its clearest note? We turn to that next.

RESONANCE RECAP—INTEGRATE

- One Breath—lengthen and deepen your exhale, blend it into all that you do.
- Two Sides—become the other, be the whole that resolves the parts.
- Three Centers—support from the hara base, and expand, open and harmonize heart and head.
- Four Energy Patterns—develop agility to sense and direct energy in any pattern and know when to sense vs. direct.

4

TUNE

S oon after I started Zen training, I was introduced to *okyo*—the chanting of sutras. I hated it. The words were an unintelligible Sanskrit, spoken quickly, and I couldn't figure out even where we were on the page, much less why we were doing this. As I knew prayer from my childhood, it was about professing beliefs or asking forgiveness. But Zen is not about beliefs or forgiveness, so what the heck were we doing? Tanouye Roshi insisted that the *okyo* not be translated into English, as the sounds would not be right. So it was something about the sound itself that made *okyo* special.

Well, it turns out that sound is quite special in terms of resonating in the human body and, in this chapter, you'll learn practices that tune the human-musical instrument that you are. Of the entire electromagnetic spectrum, from the highest frequency cosmic rays to the slowest radio waves, the two tiny bands we most easily and consciously pick up are visible light, seen with our eyes, and sound frequencies, felt with our bodies. Anyone whose been moved by pipe organs, drum circles or live concerts knows that it is not only our eardrums that vibrate to sound. In particular, vowel sounds, which abound in the Sanskrit *okyo*, resonate with energy centers from the throat to the base of the *hara*. This chapter shows ways to use the vibration of sound to shake out internal tension, much as we might shake out the dust balls in clothing pulled from the back of the closet. We'll look at ways to use vibration to open up the crucial junctions between our Three Centers where tension often constricts the free flow of energy. As we become more relaxed, less tight like a drum, a warmer, more resonant sound comes from us, perceptibly changing our communication and effect on others. What's more, as we vibrate more freely, we're able to sense more subtle energies around us. Put another way, we can increasingly tune ourselves to resonate with universal energy. That changes everything.

FINDING VOICE

I grew up with asthma in a household of smokers before anyone was connecting the dots between those two. And even after I mostly grew out of it, sore throats, colds, and bronchitis were frequent visitors. I would often get hoarse when speaking and was forever clearing my throat. I enjoyed public speaking and worked on a radio station all through high school, but whenever I heard the sound of my recorded voice, it irritated and embarrassed me; I couldn't place the problem, but it just sounded bad. As I started training in martial arts, I learned to bring out my voice in a powerful way, with loud shouts ("YAH-AY!") to punctuate sharp moves. Sometimes my voice would squeak and break, and even when it worked, I'd often end up hoarse. I was making these kind of sounds one morning at the dojo in Hawaii during a month of live-in training, punctuating every sword cut I landed atop a sort of training scarecrow called a *makiwara*. Tanouye Roshi came out on the deck and yelled at me, "Shut up! You sound like dog!" Another dressing down by the guy that lodged a fierce question in me: what's going on with my voice? I knew if my sound had been clear, he would not have stopped me.

I didn't understand the problem, much less the solution, but fortunately another aspect of Zen training was at work in my body and would eventually lead me there. It came back to that darn chanting. I couldn't stand not being able to follow along with the group *okyo* and getting lost in the Sanskrit syllables on the page, so I started memorizing them, page after page of chants. I took it one little phrase per day, and each day, added one more. I'd recite *okyo* when walking. I'd recite it cooking breakfast. I'd recite in my daily jog, which proved to be best of all because the sound of my footfall had a similar beat to the wooden drum (*mokugyo*) used in group *okyo*. And the way *okyo* is recited is very particular, which we'll pick up in the tuning exercises in just a bit. Because instead of projecting the sound out, we send it down to hit our own *hara*, with the result that the resonance increasingly comes from our whole body, not from our throat.

Because Tanouye Roshi had been a music teacher and there were a number of fine musicians and music teachers in the Hawaii dojo, *okyo* training became particularly refined. While early on, the focus is just on making a big sound bouncing off the *hara*, refinements eventually come in learning how to relax the body more deeply so as to create vertical penetration, how to blend horizontally with all the other voices, how to come in underneath them and lift them up, and even how to maintain an energetic signal in silence. Eventually, the training is to bring out your clear voice just enough, with no forced effort or extra flourish, in such a way as to perfectly accord what's going on around you. What a perfect training for learning how to resonate both true to your particular body and one with the Way. Working with voice is both a literal training in tuning our body for optimal resonance, and also a useful metaphor for how we match conditions in all of our communication and creative endeavors.

I'm not alone in having to make quite a journey to find my voice— both literally and metaphorically. I work with students all the time who, when we do loud voice work matched to sword cuts or martial art moves, can barely squeak out a sound. Gail is an example. We integrate voice work into our Zen leadership training because you can't lead if you can't be heard. Gail is normally soft-spoken, and she didn't much care for my instructions to "Send the sound of 'Yut!' with everything you've got into your *hara*," as we did overhead strikes. She went through the motions, but her "Yut" was barely above a whisper. "Louder!" I said. But little more came out. "Louder!" I pushed her again. And by this time she was getting frustrated with me, with herself, with the whole exercise. When each student in succession called out the "Yut," she could hear that her voice was nowhere near the volume of everybody else's. Afterwards she felt obliged to explain herself, "I just don't feel it's appropriate or necessary to raise my voice." I challenged her some: "What if you had to? What if there were an emergency and your voice would save people? What if you were in a situation where you had to give your all—could you do it?" It's a question you might ask yourself.

The question lodged in Gail and she wrote me about it some weeks after the program. It got her to probe her resistance to being loud, how it felt like a violation of her values, which were in line with "a gentler way to make an impact." Yet, she also could see where she needed a louder "Yut" in her life, in asserting her personal needs and not getting overloaded by others. She got curious what would have to shift in her to allow a full-bodied "Yut!" to come through her, and she started finding more of her voice.

Finding voice can be a particular challenge for women in the developed West, and even more so in other parts of the world. Veronica Ruekert in her book, *Outspoken*, points out that women speak less than men in every setting that's been studied when both are present, including the 900 most popular films between 2007 and 2016. When women do get airtime, they're up to three times more likely to be interrupted than men, even by other women. And when they speak up more than their peers, the perception of their competency goes down, whereas for men it goes up.[43] So part of the challenge in finding voice is not just speaking up or speaking more. It's having a voice that resonates, which means it matches the surrounding people and conditions.

Here again, women face more of a challenge, as our voices generally vibrate at a higher frequency than men's and become higher still when tension in the body tightens the strings. High pitched, slightly tense voices create high pitched, slightly tense reactions inside other people's bodies, and that converts into judgments like, "pushy broad," "shrill," or "hysterical." Men can get away with a little more because their voices start at a lower register, which resonates a lower, more grounded signal in the listener's body. Plus, men generally have larger bodies to work with and have often learned how to be loud without being tense. Speaking at volume without being tense is a learnable skill, but it takes practice if you're not used to it. And yes, relaxing the torso and sending sound down to bounce off the *hara* is a good way to practice. When you're in a place where you can fully let it rip, the *YAH!-AY!-TOE!* exercise gives you a chance to do just that. And if you find you can't bring out much volume, I hope, like Gail, you get curious about what's holding you back. Explore what you have to release or relax in order to bring clarity and bigness to your sound.

YAH!-AY!-TOE!

This martial art-inspired exercise gives you a chance to blast through tension with the sheer volume of sound. It's best done in a wide open space, ideally out in nature where you can let your voice vibrate into the far distance.

- **Stand with your feet shoulder width,** weight on big toes, knees soft, eyes 180-degrees.

- **YAH.** Extend your left arm in front of your face, palm toward you. Step forward with your left foot as you make an overhead chop with your right hand, landing the blade of your right hand into your left palm. At the exact moment of contact, shout the sound of "**YAH!**" down into your *hara*.

(cont.)

- **Step back** your left foot to square with your shoulders.

- **AY!** Step your left foot forward for the second chop and, as it lands, shout **"AY!"** down to your *hara*.

- **Step back.**

- **TOE!** Step forward for the third chop, timed with shouting **"TOE!"** down to your *hara*.

- **Continue in this sequence,** feeling into what can relax or open to bring greater volume or clarity to the sound. You can also drop your left hand and chop air with your right hand, but be sure to keep your chop and shout timed together.

YOU AS A MUSICAL INSTRUMENT

Imagine your body as a cello. Figure 4-1 might help your imagination along, with connections to the Three Centers we integrated in the last chapter. You might imagine emitting a clear, Yo-Yo Ma cello note as the bow is drawn across your perfectly tuned strings. Now imagine stuffing a bunch of insulation through the cello's slits and into the sound box and, while you're at it, tightening its four strings randomly. Draw the bow across and your sound is deadened and out of tune. Your voice won't be heard clearly and you won't play well with your friends in the orchestra. By the time most of us make it to adulthood, this is the body we're working with. Patterns of tension, trauma, and constriction from our life lived up until now, plus our reactions in the moment, deaden the flow and vibration of energy and throw us off pitch. How do we get the stuffing out and return our strings to their natural vibration?

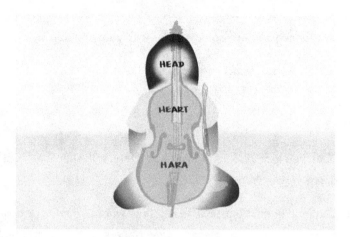

Figure 4-1. A musical instrument of Three Centers

The answer is something of a paradox: we have to relax and, at the same time, be sensitive. By being sensitive and relaxed, we become self-tuning to our environment. That doesn't mean we always like what's going on or go along with it, but we sense it clearly, which means we can vibrate with it. Just like an instrument in an orchestra, or a voice in a choir, by vibrating with others and being relaxed enough to make subtle adjustments, we come into synchrony or harmony. This is not mysterious, but simply physics: two waves reach a more stable energy state together when they match, rather than when there's interference or friction between them. Even two grandfather clocks in a room will tend to align their oscillations if they have a bit of play in their gears. So the good news is if we relax and pay attention, we'll tune ourselves to what's going on.

The bad news is that sensitivity leads to perception, which can kick off a chain reaction of thoughts, emotions, fears, conditioned tendencies, likes and dislikes, where one thing leads to another and, and before we know it, we're no longer relaxed or paying attention. This chain reaction is not inevitable. Indeed, in the next chapter we'll look at how to tame our mind not to get carried away. But first, we want to feel into how to use vibration to create a more relaxed and sensitive instrument.

Going back to our Three Centers comprising the musical instrument that is us, key places to work out tension are in the junctions between them (Figure 4-2a). The throat area often gets constricted as we try to choke back our emotions, swallow our pride, or eat our words—the idioms in our language pretty well point to what's going on. Yet this area, the fifth chakra, is key to our voice and creative expression. The solar plexus area—the third chakra and physical center of the Organizer pattern—is another prime suspect for constriction because it forms around the ego's will and efforts to control, get our arms around things, and make order out of chaos. The more we open up these junctions, the more we get energy flowing up and down through our Three Centers, which are the liberating and manifesting currents of our optimal resonance (See Figure 4-2b).

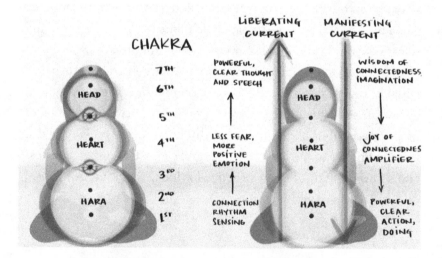

Figure 4-2. Opening the junctions, strengthening the flow of energy

Two key points of constriction in most people are between head and heart (throat, fifth chakra) and between heart and hara (solar plexus, third chakra). Opening up these and other constrictions allows for clear energy to flow through our mind-body and resonance with the energies around us.

A simple practice you could probably do right now for opening up the throat is to open your mouth as wide as possible and shut it several times. This also stimulates blood flow to the brain and creates alertness when you need it in a hurry. As you keep opening and closing your jaw, you can add to this gently tapping on the outside of your throat and neck area with soft fists. You'll feel a warmth and softness come into this area.

To create some opening in the solar plexus area, use your fingertips to feel where your ribcage comes together near your midline. Feeling along the underside of the ribcage, starting near the center, gently tuck your fingers under and in. Don't press too hard (there's a slip of bone in here and you don't want to break it). You just want to hold some muscles in place while you take a huge, deep breath and then let out a sigh of relief. Move your fingers slightly laterally on the ribcage and do it again. Repeat several times, moving along the underside of the ribcage, each time letting the bigness and release of your breath tease apart tension in this area.

To engage more vibration in opening these constricting suspects, I highly recommend the *Blahs* and *Empty Throat* exercises that follow. These and other exercises are also available as videos at https://resonatethebook.com. Credit here to Betsy Wetzig for introducing me to the Blahs; she recognized my Organizer tightness and showed me this terrific practice for loosening it up. And yes, I do this one every morning, too.

VIBRATING THE JUNCTIONS:
BLAHS AND EMPTY THROAT

Blahs

a. **Lie on your back** with your knees bent, arms straight up in the air at the level of your shoulders (Figure 4-3a).

b. **Lift one shoulder** off the floor, stretching through the fingertips of that hand. Bring it down and do the same on the other side.

c. **Alternate left and right** arm extensions, with the energy coming from your spine out through your fingertips.

d. **Exhale the sound of "BLAHHHHH"** as your alternating arms pick up speed, vibrating the midline of the body (Figure 4-3b).

e. **Repeat several times** with the sense of shaking out tension, letting it exit through your fingertips.

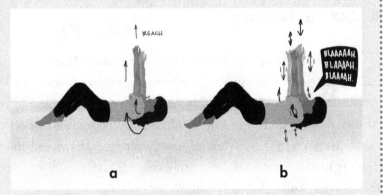

Figure 4-3. Getting rid of the blahs

(cont.)

Empty Throat

a. **Lie on your back** with your knees bent, hands on your *hara*.

b. **Breathe in deeply,** feeling the *hara* expand, and connect your big toes to the earth on the exhale. Keep breathing deeply to and from *hara* throughout the exercise.

c. **Exhale a long "OH" sound from your *hara*,** with the throat completely open and unemployed, as if the sound came from the *hara* itself, and simply passed through the wide-open throat.

d. **Exhale a long "AHHH" sound from your *hara*,** again, passing unobstructed through your wide-open throat. This sound will also vibrate away tension in your solar plexus.

e. **Exhale a long "EEEE" sound from your *hara*,** letting the throat remain completely relaxed and empty, even as you feel the sound of "EEEE" vibrating within it.

MUSIC OF THE CHAKRAS

With some of the constriction between centers freed up, we're ready to tune our whole musical instrument self, top-to-bottom and bottom-to-top. Anodea Judith, in her comprehensive guide to the chakras, *Eastern Body Western Mind*, lays out the sounds associated with each chakra.[44] These aren't arbitrary assignments. Instead, Judith explains how each sound frequency sets off a vibration centered around a particular chakra. The more you practice with the music of the chakras, the more you'll feel these connections in your own body. Vowel sounds vibrate primarily in the body cavities. At a given pitch, "OH" has the lowest frequency, vibrating at the base of the *hara* (first chakra). As you may have just felt in the last exercises, the epicenter of "AH" is the solar plexus (third chakra), while "EE" vibrates in the throat (fifth chakra). Consonant sounds are higher frequency still, and the two that vibrate most in the sixth and seventh chakras are "MM" and "NG" respectively. Figure 4-4 shows the sounds of each chakra and is a guide to the exercises that follow.

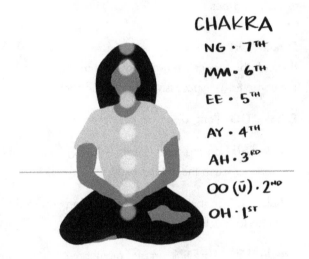

CHAKRA

NG · 7ᵀᴴ

MM · 6ᵀᴴ

EE · 5ᵀᴴ

AY · 4ᵀᴴ

AH · 3ᴿᴰ

OO (ū) · 2ᴺᴰ

OH · 1ˢᵀ

Figure 4-4. Sounds of the chakras

Even if you can't do the full *Music of the Chakras* exercise right now, you can get a feel for the association of sound with your body by exhaling the sound of "OH," followed by "OO" (long U), feeling both deep in your *hara*. Next do "AH" and "AY" feeling how they vibrate higher up, in the solar plexus and heart areas. Next do "EE," "MM" and "NG," feeling how the sound moves into the throat, middle and top of your head, respectively. If and when you can engage the *Music of the Chakras* exercise, you'll get a chance to feel the deeper work of vibration and the two energy currents that liberate what's stuck bottom-up, and manifest what's ready to happen top-down.

MUSIC OF THE CHAKRAS

Lying Down—Lie on your back with your knees bent, big toes connected to the earth, hands on your *hara*. Let your body relax into the floor and make all sounds with a relaxed, empty throat. Keep eyes 180-degrees.

a. **Exhale "OH"** at full volume, letting the sound stretch out through the longest, slowest exhale that is comfortable. Do the same for on successive breaths for each of the sounds.

b. **Exhale "OO" (long U)** on the next breath.

c. **Exhale "AH"** on the third breath, moving your right hand up hand to touch the solar plexus.

d. **Exhale "AY"** on the fourth breath, moving your right hand up hand to touch the midline at heart level.

e. **Exhale "EE"** on the fifth breath, moving your right hand up hand to touch the throat.

f. **Exhale "MM"** on the sixth breath, moving your right hand up hand to touch the face.

g. **Exhale "NG"** on the seventh breath, moving your right hand above the top of your head, feeling lift through the top-back of your head.

h. **On one, long exhale, transition through all seven sounds starting from the base:** "OH-OO-AH-AY-EE-MM-NG" This is the liberating current from bottom up.

i. **On one long exhale, transition through all seven sounds starting from the top:** "NG-MM-EE-AY-AH-OO-OH" This is the manifesting current from top down.

(cont.)

Standing—Same as a-i above, but start with the **6-point check:**

1. Weight in big toes
2. Knees soft
3. *Hara* expanded and naturally weighted in gravity, hands on *hara*
4. Heart open, shining straightforward, aligned in gravity
5. Eyes 180-degrees
6. Inhale expanding the *hara*, Let gravity guide the exhale slowly down through *hara* and big toes.

VOICE RECLAIMED

Tuning our body with the vibration of sound is not a quick fix. It is deep, patient work. Yet it doesn't require another day at the fitness center or new piece of equipment. You have what you need to work with at all times. It calls only for an intentionality to keep expanding the moments where you become one-with breath, send sound down to a relaxed, receiving *hara*, and release any tension along the way. As Loehr and Schwartz share in the *Power of Full Engagement,* one of the best practices for sustaining our energy through a long workday is to take brief breaks about every ninety minutes[45]. Breath and sound exercises lend themselves well to five minutes of practice here or there.

What's at stake is nothing less than reclaiming your full vibrant voice and all that you would creatively give voice to. Anodea Judith finds this center associated not only with speaking but being heard—i.e., resonant communication with others. It's also tied to creative expression and being able to put feelings and ideas into words[46]. Sometimes, as we tune ourselves, the changes are so subtle that we may think nothing is happening. And, just as when resonance hits a tipping point and an entirely new state is possible, sometimes the changes are profound.

After memorizing the *okyo*, and repeating it daily for years, I grew to love its sounds, and the feeling of them coming through me like an amplified heartbeat. During *sesshin* when I could do *okyo* with a group, I could start to play with ways to make my voice work in others and their voices in me. And the more my body relaxed, the more I could feel the great sea of vibration in our collective sound, with no separation or conscious effort—just pure vibration vibrating me to play along. I understood why Tanouye Roshi used to say *okyo* was a great training for inducing the boundary-free zone that is Samadhi.

About eight years after Tanouye's "barking dog" scolding, I was sitting in *sesshin* at the Spring Green Dojo, now training with Gordon Greene Roshi. It was the dead of winter, and we were sitting in a small cabin, heated by a woodstove that was working overtime. We were deep in a sit, coming up on a time, called *sanzen*, when we would do our one-on-one *koan* training with Gordon. Suddenly, in the depth of meditation, a great internal heat rose toward my head with a constriction in my throat that felt like I was being strangled. I felt the urge to scream, but breathed it down as deeply as I could, as the constriction grew tighter and something absolutely had to give. The bell rang announcing *sanzen* and I shot out the door. Gordon had chosen an outside platform for this morning's *sanzen*, and as I started my jog toward it, violent, full-bodied screams were coming out of my body, as if expelling a serpent—I can't describe it any other way. My body went through the motions it knew without thought, as I approached Gordon on the platform, and out came another thundering shout, matched exactly by Gordon's own shout. In perfect resonance, we understood each other completely.

Some months later, a dear friend of mine who's known me since high school commented, "I notice you don't clear your throat anymore." Neither am I irritated by the sound of my recorded voice. I don't get sick or hoarse as often, nor do I doubt that whatever is mine to create will be given voice.

Whatever you have to do: reclaim your true voice.

TWENTY-ONE-BREATH SALUTATION

A final tuning exercise to share with you has been inspired by several sources[47] and puts together exercises you're already familiar with if you've been playing along. When we do this exercise in Zen leadership programs, people often have the experience of opening into a Samadhi state of pure connectedness, a feeling of being space, being time, being whole. I don't tell you this as a guarantee, but only so you don't underestimate what's possible for you. As you might imagine, opening into Samadhi is exactly the condition in which we resonate one-with the entire context. The awkwardness of a separate "I" drops away, as we slip seamlessly into the Way. Nancy Trivellato likens it to an out-of-body experience[48], and I understand why she makes that connection. But I would say it is a liberated body experience where we have resolved the Two Sides of universal energy played through this particular body. Or, as Jill Bolte Taylor put it in *My Stroke of Insight* after a debilitating stroke had temporarily wiped out her sense of a separate self: "We are the power of the universe with manual dexterity."[49]

Likewise, we do well to temporarily wipe out our sense of a separate self and experience our intrinsic connectedness, and fortunately there are ways short of a stroke for doing that. I encourage you to immerse yourself in this exercise—*21-Breath Salutation*—for maybe twenty minutes, and come back to it again and again. Once you have the hang of it, a follow-on, more advanced version can be found on https://resonatethebook.com.

21-BREATH SALUTATION

This exercise is done **lying down**, best with legs extended and big toes able to press against a vertical surface as in the Three Center exercise of Chapter 3. Alternatively, you can bend your knees and connect the big toes into the earth as in Music of the Chakras.

As you begin, establish the **rhythm of your *hara* breathing**, as in the Three Center exercise: exhale slowly down through your *hara* and gently press your big toes against a surface. Release and relax on the inhale, fully expanding the *hara*. **Exhale as long and slowly** as comfortably possible.

The exercise starts with twenty-one breaths, three at each of the seven chakras, starting from the base of the *hara*—first chakra—and working up to the crown of the head—seventh chakra.

- **On the first breath:** Send the **sound** of that chakra **down vertically** to it and through it, down to your feet, opening the unobstructed flow of energy through the chakra, same as you did in the Music of the Chakras exercise (See Figure 4-5a). For example, exhale **"OH"** on the first breath, opening the first chakra.

- **On the second breath:** Send the sound of that chakra out; imagine **horizontally expanding** the chakra into the space around it, like waves expanding from a central drop of water, but in all dimensions. (Figure 4-5b).

- **On the third breath:** Silently connect with the **emotion of this bigness**, e.g., gratitude, reverence, peace, joy, or whatever you feel (Figure 4-5c).

Continue working up each chakra, spending three breaths at each, where the first two use sound and the third is silent. Exhale the following sounds down on the first breath at the second through

(cont.)

seventh chakras: **"OO"** (long U), **"AH," "AY," "EE," MM," "NG."**

After twenty-one breaths, rest in this state for several minutes, **feeling your whole body and the space around it all at once.** Once one you're able to consistently reach twenty-one breaths without losing your concentration, go can go onto the advanced form of this exercise available at https://resonatethebook.com.

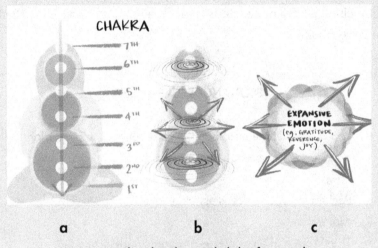

Figure 4-5. Three breaths at each chakra for vertical, horizontal, and emotional connection

Integrated and tuned, our body increasingly vibrates with the energy that is ours to create with, and increasingly helps us build resonance with others. Now we're ready to tackle the final challenge of operating our Universal Energy Concentrator, namely the mind of its own that it came with. The good news is that our mind can keep evolving as our body matures through stages of development, for example: building empathy, becoming rational, reconciling multiple points of view, sensing its connectedness and being able to witness itself. The bad news is that at each stage, it confronts habits already embedded from earlier in life, and can always regress to its self-centered roots. Even when we're not being triggered into our survivalist instincts, the very process of sensing and perception, which is key to building resonance, is a thought stirrer-upper. It's easy for our mind to get carried away by the embodied thought, emotion and habit loops of the past, and here we go, swinging from one thought to the next in so-called "monkey-mind." Without taming the mind, it's a fear-triggered, endlessly chattering beast. Tame it, and it can embrace and include all the bigness it is now capable of growing into. That's our next mission.

RESONANCE RECAP—TUNE

- You are a musical instrument, pulled out of tune by tension and stuck-ness, brought into tune by relaxation and energy flow.
- Reclaiming your voice is essential to being heard and creative expression.
- The throat and solar plexus are particularly prone to constriction and are good areas to relax and open.
- The vibration of sound helps tune the body; a good practice is to exhale the sound associated with each chakra.
- Vertical energy flow combined with horizontal expansion is a gateway to Samadhi: feeling the entire body at once merged with the whole picture.
- When we're in Samadhi, we're tuned to the Way.

5

TAME

Bethany's bare hands raised the top bar of the hive to check for queen cells. She's not a beekeeper by profession—she's a physician—yet it's often in nature that she sees the effects of her Zen training in how it changes her resonance. As she lifted the intricate honeycomb out of the hive, several drones crawled onto her hands as others danced around her head. She breathed. They hummmmmed. She listened, having learned that subtle changes in the hive's frequency could signal distress. The hive began to bellow. "I held perfectly still and took a *hara* breath," she recalls. "And another. The roar subsided. I carefully replaced the comb, no sign yet of an impending colony divide. I walked slowly out of the orchard to permit any hitchhikers a chance to detach from my clothes and return home at their own pace."

"When I first started tending hives on our property fifteen months ago," Bethany recounts, "the accoutrements were bountiful: bee suit, gloves, smoker. With each visit to the hive I outfitted myself, a warrior preparing for battle. I soon found the bulky gear a hindrance, an artificial barrier preventing me from sensing and engaging with the hive. As I shed layer upon layer of protection, I became more aware of subtle shifts made by the colony. I, in turn, could respond to their ever-changing needs. No one needs to sting. No one needs to get stung."

This stripping away of layers that affords a much more direct and responsive engagement with life is a good metaphor for how Zen tames us not to be docile, but to be one-with. As Bethany puts it, "Through Zen training, I might shed the manufactured layers of guilt, frustration, materialism, and ego that prevent me from sensing and engaging with the world, elevating my sensitivity to the vibration of others, and enabling me to respond in measure."

To function seamlessly with what life presents, making our own difference without flourish or sting, is to accord the Way. And it calls for a mind that has been tamed beyond endlessly proving or protecting itself, or carelessly provoking others. This chapter builds on practices you've already learned, and adds some core elements of Zen training by which we can convert this mind-of-its-own that our Universal Energy Concentrator came with from being a tyrant to a tool. In particular, we learn how to tame the impulses, fears and egocentricity that were already embodied habits before either of us could read this sentence. We lay out the central practice of Zen—*Zazen* or sitting meditation—by which we tame the mind through the body, including re-wiring the brain. We'll also explore some milestones or stages along the path of practice. These stages in Zen training can feel like a match between our local, ego self trying to get its needs met, wrestling with something wildly bigger—our whole Self—emerging.

How far you go along the path of practice is, of course, up to you. What I can assure you is that taming your mind and body to clear resistance and vibrate freely is a most worthy battle. For beyond the resistance lies a wondrous possibility: not only do we resonate with universal energy, but it increasingly functions through us.

ENTER ZEN

I hadn't been training in Zen very long before it became clear that something inside was deeply resisting. I recall hearing a lecture Tanouye Roshi gave in Chicago that seared into me some unforgettable truths. But I had just been offered a job at NASA—a chance to pursue my childhood dream to be an astronaut! Something in me feared that Zen would take away my dream or make my life unrecognizable. I remember thinking: *I know what you're saying is true—it's all a delusion—but please give me this one more delusion before I accept it.*

Life happily accommodated my request. Still, Tanouye Roshi's words that night played in my head more loudly than my usual mind chatter. One of his statements was: "Sit twenty minutes a day; it will change your life." *I'm a scientist,* I thought, *I will run this experiment.* I wasn't ready to commit my life to some kind of full-blown immersion into Zen—whatever that meant. But surely I could sit twenty minutes a day and see what would happen. And what happened was wonderful; it made me more effective at work, more calm, more able to see myself in the moment and better able to choose my behavior. It made me more successful. While I never made it onto the astronaut roster, I rose quickly through NASA's management ranks, eventually becoming the Deputy Manager for integrating the Space Station. I'm sure Zen can do good things for your résumé, too.

But at some point, everything still fell apart. A painful divorce, a terrible boss, the death of a close friend, and the final extinguishing of my astronaut dream all conspired to get me asking *What the hell is my life about anyway?* I no longer cared about protecting the contours of my life because it all sucked. Around that time, one of my Aikido students wanted to attend *sesshin,* something I had been avoiding for years. I felt shamed into going with him and did so, full of trepidation. I knew the hours of sitting would be long; I knew my legs would get sore. What I didn't know was that in four days of *sesshin,* I would learn more about myself than I had in my entire life up to that point. On the second full day of training, the mind-chattering television set in my head completely stopped. Up to that point, I didn't even know it had an off-switch. The peace that flooded through me was so deep and pervasive that when I came back to thinking, I knew I would do this training for the rest of my life. I dove in.

I entered Zen. Which is to say, I reached a point where, instead of using Zen to make my life-as-I-knew-it better, I was ready to let the training change me, knowing life would never be the same. Of course, this was exactly what my ambitious, dream-pursuing ego had been afraid of all along. I'll add to this story later, but I tee it up now so you know that, in most cases, entering Zen happens in stages—these past few paragraphs took me a good five years. Know also that the benefits begin from the start. I've seen many people experience benefits they describe as life-changing in the space of a few days. And know that if you hear a niggling voice of doubt in your head wondering how much of this Zen stuff you can do without it changing the contours of your life beyond what you, strictly speaking, asked for, well, that's natural, too.

So what is this sitting practice that even in twenty-minute-a-day doses is so powerful as to change one's life? You already know many of its contours, as we've been building toward it from the start with deep *hara* breathing, 180-degree vision, alignment in gravity, and an ability to be one-with our breath, giving each breath a count. Basic instructions for *Zazen* practice are pulled together in the box and a video is also available at https://resonatethebook.com. Still, this guidance cannot match the value of working with an instructor live or sitting with a group, something available to you in any IZL program, if not closer. I encourage you to pause in your reading and try this practice for ten to twenty minutes, especially if you're not already familiar with *Zazen*, as your own experience will give you much better context for the sections that follow.

ZAZEN—SITTING MEDITATION

Choose a space relatively free of clutter, away from cell phones and other distractions, where you are unlikely to be interrupted during your time of sitting. While eventually it's possible to sit in challenging and distracting conditions, early on, optimize what you can.

Establish the base. Sit either on a chair as in the Sitting Integration exercise (of Chapter 3), or on a wedge of cushions. In either case, establish a stable, tripod base—tailbone and big toes (Figure 5-1a) or tailbone and two knees (Figure 5-1b)—where the hip joints are slightly higher than the knees. If you're sitting on cushions and your knees cannot make contact with the ground, you can roll towels or place smaller cushions under the knees to give them support. Align the torso in gravity so that weight drops evenly through all three points of your tripod base.

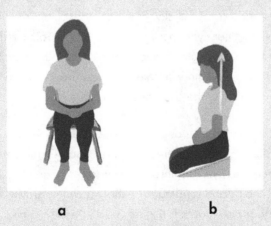

a   b

Figure 5-1. *Zazen*—Establish a stable, tripod base

Hand position. Take the first knuckle of your left thumb into your right hand and bend that knuckle so that your left fingers overlay the right (Figure 5-2). With your hands in this position, hold your arms out in front of you, rounded as if hugging a tree.

(cont.)

Keeping this roundedness, bring them down and rest the blades of your hands on your *hara*, rolling your shoulders down and back. This hand position may feel odd at first until your muscles get used to it. But in time, you'll appreciate how it ties together breath and body and keeps your torso aligned in gravity.

Figure 5-2. *Zazen* hand position

Eyes and suspension. Let your eyes expand to 180-degree vision, splashing off the floor a couple of yards or meters in front of you. Feel a slight lift from the back-top of your head as if suspended by a fine thread from the sky. Feel how that sense of suspension relaxes and lengthens your neck and back, slightly rotating the pelvis. Keep this sense of length through your spine; as the nape of the neck lengthens, the chin will naturally tuck. Empty any tension this lengthening puts into the chest or solar plexus area.

Breathing. Breathing in through your nose, draw an inhale down into your hara, letting it expand freely (Figure 5-3a). Gently set the *hara* by extending energy down through your tailbone and knees (or big toes, if on chair), and sending the exhale down in gravity, as slowly and deeply as comfortable. (Figure 5-3b). As exhale ends, release and relax the *hara* to draw in a fresh inhale, expanding the *hara* again. Set and slowly exhale down. The downward exhale, maybe four times longer than the inhale, will add countervailing lift to the back-top of the head. In your mind's voice, blend each breath with a count, starting at one. When you get to ten, or if you lose your count, go back to one.

(cont.)

No Movement. Aside from slight adjustments in gravity if your posture has slipped, do not move or fidget once you've started a sit. As the impulse to move arises, blend it with your breath, similar to any other thought. Akin to 180-degree vision, open all of your senses softly, without sharp focus. Pour your entire self into your breathing, and let breath do the work of managing any emotions or thoughts that arise.

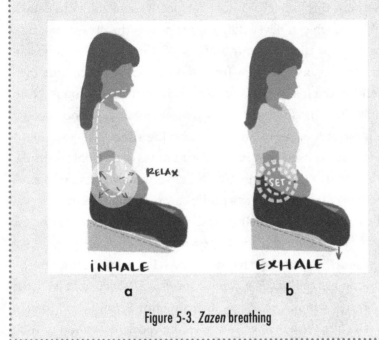

INHALE   EXHALE

a   b

Figure 5-3. *Zazen* breathing

TAME IMPULSES

I don't know anyone who sits down in *Zazen* for the first time and finds it totally natural. Rather, it almost always rubs up against a comfortable habit that starts asserting itself, as in, "Hey, who says I can't move? My eyebrow is itching right now and I'll move if I damn well feel like it." So, what's with the not moving and how on earth does this help us resonate better? Well, what we're doing by not moving is interrupting old, reflexive loops. Every time we watch an impulse and don't act on it, we're strengthening a self-regulation circuit between the prefrontal cortex and the midbrain. Basically, we're re-wiring the brain. In fact, sit long enough and you'll build a superhighway of self-regulation that lets you see impulses and choose them or not, see emotions, rather than get swept away by them, and see yourself able to make all these choices[50].

Without this crucial Witness perspective and ability to detach from habits, we can never fully resonate with the present because the past keeps dictating our actions. Without anyone imposing constraints on our freedom from the outside, we steal our own freedom on the inside when we won't challenge these loops. Now, you may think brushing an itchy eyebrow is hardly a loop needing to be interrupted, yet by starting in on the simple, obvious loops that present themselves in even a few minutes of motionless sitting, we're building the capacity to detach from our most ingrained habits.

Bethany described this as a peeling away of "manufactured layers of guilt, frustration, materialism, and ego." A feeling of guilt arises, for example (*What am I doing sitting here? I should be doing something more productive.*), and we breathe through it, letting it come and go. Frustration arises (*This is a complete waste of time!*), and we let it pass through without acting on it. Distraction arises (*Wind coming up. Did I close the window? That window needs replacing. . . . Who was the person we called last time? I didn't like that guy. . . . What number am I on?*), and we go back to one. This increased capacity is now available as we face into everyday decisions. *Do I take this shortcut? Spend more time on social media? Speak up at this meeting?* Based on our past, we may have tendencies toward "yes" or "no" in any of these cases, but we tune ourselves more to the real needs of the present only when we're free of knee-jerk reactions from the past.

Another source of discomfort I often hear is around: Why do I have to keep my eyes open? It's much easier if I shut them. And surely there are many forms of meditation that do just that. So I don't say it's wrong, but it's not optimal for creating a state of complete awareness and complete relaxation at the same time, which is the condition we're building in *Zazen*. In a way, it *is* easier to relax and focus on the inside when we shut our eyes to the outside. But it's also easier to drift off, becoming less aware and closer to a dream state. It also leaves our visual cortex—a huge portion of the brain that accounts for about a third of its energy consumption—out of the brain-training game. Instead, we want to be able to register visual perceptions, along with any other sense, and not let them drive us impulsively into loops of thought, emotion and action. It's a huge miss to leave out of this training what, for most people, is their dominant sense. So, yes, I know it's less comfortable initially, and yet it adds a crucial component to the re-wiring of our brain.

TAME FEARS

Fear and all of its emotional cousins—sadness, anger, disgust, shame, joy and excitement—are meditated in the midbrain. As we saw earlier, our emotional state is also broadcast through hormonal release from the midbrain into the bloodstream, affecting not only the functioning of our heart, but the strength and coherence of our electromagnetic field and the "vibe" others pick up from us. When we're on high alert, we resonate "high alert" to everyone around us.

Fear is tamed by connections from the prefrontal cortex which squirts what acts as a fear-retardant (GABA) onto the midbrain (amygdala). These are among the connections strengthened through sitting meditation, giving some underpinning to the subjective experience of meditators who consistently report decreased fear and depression, more positive emotions, faster recovery from stress, and greater emotional equanimity[51].

At the subjective level, this equanimity builds when we are able to sit with difficult emotions, which will certainly arise during *Zazen*, and allow those emotions to run their course without amplifying or acting on them. It builds by sitting with physical discomfort, and not running away. A kind of deep courage develops that sees how all this stuff arises and falls away like so many images on a screen, while resting as the screen itself.

We can apply the same "not running away" discipline we cultivate in *Zazen* to further tame our fears by facing into them. Fears, as we've seen, derive from basic human needs such as to be safe, loved, respected, or authentic. And, as Arthur Janov reminds us, it's not uncommon for those needs to function without natural fill lines, particularly if they've become substitutes for another unmet need. So we can lose track of what's enough. Indeed, "never enough" and "having it all" are sometimes the battle cries of the ambitious, as if that kind of living were sustainable. But "never enough" is never sustainable and will sooner or later lead to fear: an isolated ego struggling to fill an unfillable hole. And since we have more than one need, if any one of them is an unfillable hole, it distorts our focus and creates real deficiencies in meeting other needs (much less the needs of others). For example, if I have an insatiable craving for money in order to feel safe, I may never open myself to love, belonging, or authentic self-expression.

But the discipline of *Zazen* instills a visceral, vibration-matching sense of "just enough." We feel into what's just enough effort to set the *hara* and not tense unnecessary muscles. We feel into what's just enough effort to lengthen our exhale, letting gravity do most of the work. When we're doing walking meditation with a group, we feel into what's just enough speed to join seamlessly with the group. When eating, we take just enough food to sustain our energy. When going to the bathroom, use just enough toilet paper. When bathing, use just enough water. And so on. Look at your own life and you'll see countless opportunities to cultivate this sense of "just enough." What's just enough speed to merge onto this expressway? What's just enough food to keep this body strong and healthy? These are rhythms or fill lines we can sense.

The stronger our sense of "just enough," the more we're matching the conditions around us—i.e., the more we're resonating harmoniously rather than clomping around like a bull in a china shop. We're also building a key tool for taming our fears, because fears connect to needs—as depicted in Figure 5-4. If we can trace the root of a fear to the need we're afraid won't be met, we can ask: *what's just enough of this need? What's enough love? Enough authenticity? Enough safety?* In many cases, we'll know we already have enough, and can relax into realizing that we don't have to contort this situation to further meet our need (e.g. *I'm safe enough. I don't need more money to feel safe*). In some cases, we'll see the need is asserting itself for good reason and it needs to inform something within our power to act (e.g., *I'm not safe enough. I need to cut expenses and save more for the future*). If the answer is "never enough" we know we're dealing with a neurotic, proxy need that we do well to acknowledge without acting on it (e.g., *I never feel safe enough, there's never enough money; this is old and deep in me*). And where do or did we learn how to acknowledge difficult emotions without running away or not acting on them? In *Zazen*.

If you'd like to pick a fear to tame, the *Taming Fear* exercise is a good one to practice. In addition to the joy of freeing yourself from residual fears, you'll find the benefits of this practice resonates to others, as they sense in you the growing strength of fearlessness.

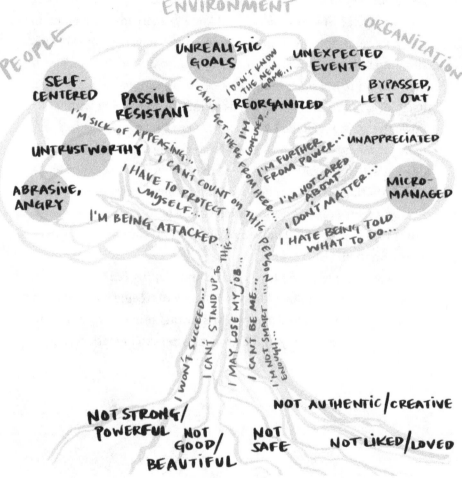

Figure 5-4. Many triggers, common roots

TAMING FEAR

- **Focus** on something or someone that triggers you into anger or some other difficult emotional state. It could be one of the "fruits" of the tree in Figure 5-4, triggered by people in your life or the environment you work in. It could be a characteristic of a family member or co-worker, or something going on in the world that drives you crazy. You'll find this exercise most fruitful if you pick some triggering situation you have some power to affect. I recommend writing it down so you can focus on one thing clearly, then ask yourself, *So what? What impact does this have on me personally?* Normally, we're used to externalizing our irritations and wrapping stories around what will happen. But in this exercise, go internal. Ask yourself: *What do I fear may be true about me?*

- **Get to the Root.** And then ask again: *So what?* What may that lead to, in your worst nightmares? Keep asking *so what* until you get to the root, and see if you recognize it as one of the roots in Figure 5-4. Most likely it's one of them, but feel free to add to the root system if necessary. Tracing these otherwise unconscious pathways within us is the first step to being free of their silent control.

- **Ask "What's Enough?"** Focusing now on this root, ask yourself: *How do I sense when I've had enough (of meeting this need)? How do I know that I don't have enough now?* If you're drawing a blank, good chance this is one of those unfillable needs. Likewise, if you keep arriving to this root from a number of different triggers, it probably has no fill line. Good to know. Even if you have a sense of what's enough and being in a deficit state, good to know that, too.

- **Relax and center.** Let out a long, slow exhale and relax into your *hara*. Feel into this root fear and imagine moving into it. Get

(cont.)

closer. Become that fear. Feel into where that fear shows up in your body as tightness, heaviness, like a sealed safe, or whatever. Enter those places with your breath awareness. Take your time with this step, as you're using mind-as-breath to direct the flow of energy into places that are not vibrating freely, exploring what might free up. Let every emotion that surfaces run through you, stabilized by your deep *hara* breathing.

- **Acknowledge** the fear, accept that it's a fear operating in you, perhaps deep and old, perhaps insatiable. Notice the awareness with which you see the fear is not, itself, afraid. Become the fear and there is no longer a separate self to be afraid. Rest in that awareness.

- **Find your power to act.** Neither fighting nor fleeing, being the fear, how can you extend your energy, your gifts, your best effort, into this situation? If this need had no power over you, what would be your best way forward?

TAME EGOCENTRICITY

We all grew up through an egocentric stage of development. Some of us still spend a lot of time there, and all of us can regress there, especially under stress. As a stage of development, egocentricity is a natural fact. But if we can't tame it and transcend it as adults, from the point of view of resonance, it saddles us with two enormous problems. First, it inhibits our ability to resonate with others and get them resonating with us. Second, it inhibits our ability to resonate with universal energy, even as it steals our sense of identity, convincing us we're more limited and separate than we actually are.

Zen training can lift us out of this egocentricity by subjecting the ego to a form where it simply cannot do its own thing. For example, when eating during a Zen training, not only do we take just enough for ourselves, but look into the pot of whatever's being served to make sure there's just enough for everyone, and then adjust our own portion accordingly. Eating during training is not an individual act of pickiness and preference, but eating whatever's served and falling in with the rhythm of the group. Since eating is one of the earliest and oldest habits we develop, you can imagine that even in this wonderfully nourishing part of the training, we run into deep and old stuff.

When Gordon Greene was just a new priest and doing live-in training under Tanouye Roshi in Hawaii, one of the things he recalls was the mandate to always serve others first. No matter how exhausted he was, how hard he had worked all day, or how little sleep he had gotten the night before, if someone came to the dojo, Gordon had to take of care them. From making them tea, to helping them train, to making sure they were safe on the property, he put their needs above his own. What this repeated practice did over time was not only stretch his capacity, but also bring him into resonance with people, something which, if he could climb into this sentence he would say, he dearly wanted to learn. It did something else, too. The more we resonate with others—remember, we're making internal maps of them as we go—the more we're experiencing another aspect of our whole Self, not just the usual suspect ego. And we're learning more how to use the ego as a tool, not as the point and purpose of our life.

So this taming of ego is not about learning to be a nice, kind, generous person—a bunch of laudable terms the ego would love to take credit for. No. It's about opening toward our whole Self. Every person we serve is a part of us. Every situation we serve is a part of us. Becoming one-with each, no separation—no bee suit, gloves and smoker—we merge with each directly. And in that process, mind is increasingly freed from the ego as its defining identity. Some would call it selflessness, but you could just as easily say it's selfishness on the grandest scale: being whole Selfish, not local selfish.

You don't have to be in a Zen dojo to practice this. Opportunities are always present to stretch beyond your usual suspect self and toward your whole Self and act from this place of connected expansiveness. Two readily available practices follow (*Whole beyond the Ego*), and I invite you into the relaxed joy of seeing what happens when you put them into practice.

WHOLE BEYOND THE EGO

Serve others first. A polished host makes a practice of serving others first with food or drink. Explore ways to apply this same spirit to interactions with others when you start to feel yourself tightening into a small, selfish space. For example, if you're pushing an idea or point of view in a conversation, pause and feel into what serves the other person, and frame a question or opening that helps you sense what serves, rather than what you want to sell. If you're vying for that one-car advantage in a lane-merge on an expressway, pause and feel into letting the other go first. Notice what has to shift in you to serve others first.

Act for the Whole Picture. In important matters or decisions, make it a practice to step back from your usual perspective to see it from multiple perspectives, culminating in seeing and acting as the whole picture. A simple way to play with this, adapted from *The Zen Leader*, is to imagine concentric circles around your local self perspective, as in Figure 5-5a. For the matter at hand, fill in a few names of people or groups most directly affected in the inner circle. In the outer circle, add names or groups indirectly affected (Figure 5-5b).

- **Start with your local perspective.** What's in your personal interest?

- **Widen the net.** One at a time, drop into the names in your inner and outer circle and become them, using empathy and imagination. How is this matter in their interest? What's their advice to you?

(cont.)

• **End with the Whole self.** Imagine embracing and including all these perspectives and what's best for the whole picture. Speaking as the whole picture, how does this matter serve the whole? What's your best advice to your local self?

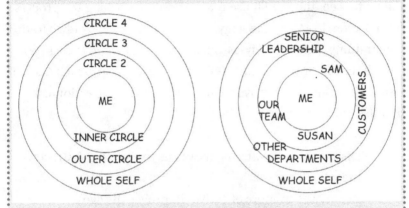

Figure 5-5. From local self to whole Self

Source: G. Whitelaw, The Zen Leader, pp 233-234.
Used with permission.

THE TAMING PROCESS

As you might imagine, the ego develops something of a love-hate relationship with the taming process of Zen. It loves meditation for the positive effects it starts sensing in its life: better concentration, peacefulness, resilience, immune response, stress recovery, and positive emotions—to name just a few of the well-researched outcomes. But it hates meditation for the disruption and challenge it starts making to the ego's world. So, the ego is not the best judge of whether our training is making any progress. Plus, we know that resonance to a new state is generally preceded by repeated stimulation whose effects are hidden. This calls for patience and trust in the process, which is made easier when we have a map of the territory.

So, here I offer a somewhat simplified, personalized map of how taming the ego unfolds, hammering us into an instrument that increasingly resonates with the Way. This taming process is not unique to Zen, though I'll use that word in describing the process. I'm not referring to an ideology or belief system, but rather to the deep training of mind-body-as-one. Moreover, this process is never smooth, linear, or once-and-for-all. But like a choppy stock market with a discernible trend over time, a nominal progression can be identified as follows:

1. Disturbance or suffering moves us toward Zen (attracts the ego).
2. Zen makes us more effective (improves the ego).
3. Zen makes us more aware (expands the ego).
4. Awareness makes us more awake, gives us glimpses, stirs our innate longing to be whole (challenges the ego).
5. We dive in to lose this clumsy separateness, this prison of self (assaults the ego)
6. We see all the way through (reframes the ego).
7. We realign around our insight, trigger by trigger, until it is embodied (reorganizes the ego).
8. We freely, fully express who we are (uses the ego).

Here's what you're likely to run into at each stage:

Attracts the ego. Something drives us toward Zen. In my own case, I wanted to get to the bottom of things—the same kind of urge that took me into physics, philosophy, and spiritual disciplines; a need to comprehend *what is this all about?* I was also highly ambitious and wanted to be perfect in all things (masking a deep insecurity, I might add). When my Aikido teacher told me Zen training would be key to reaching the peak of my game, something in me stirred. So, between trying to get to the bottom of things or the top of my game, or some other extreme, I was drawn to Zen—albeit tentatively at first. Something in me resonated with the simplicity and clarity of Zen, with Zen teachers, Zen art, Zen-influenced martial arts—all of it.

Often the disturbance that draws us toward training is brought on by suffering: a loved one lost, a debilitating setback. Or we may have a burning question we need to get to the bottom of: *How do I handle all this? What really matters anyway? Are we all just going to struggle and then die?* This disturbance is a form of what in Zen is called "Great Doubt," and it not only initiates our journey, but accompanies us all the way through.

Improves the ego. Good news, things get better. One of the first gifts of my Zen training was learning to breathe more deeply, which, given my asthmatic beginnings, was revolutionary. A deeply felt anxiety started settling down. I could concentrate better. I was more settled and effective at work. The Zen toolkit and practices I've shared with you really do improve effectiveness.

The danger of this improved effectiveness is that we may mistake it as the point of Zen, and start using Zen, or any form of training, as something like a non-prescription drug to make matters more comfortable for the ego. My own life has shown me this danger. I used to have an irregular heartbeat that would race and cause me all kinds of trouble. Once I learned that I could slow down my heart by slowing down my exhale, I was able to manage my heartbeat into a more regular range. I'd use this technique to get through a difficult day or even an astronaut candidate physical. But what I wasn't doing was listening to what my heart was trying to tell me, namely that my life was screwed up. By using meditation as a coping technique, I put off the truth for a long time. Which meant things had to get worse.

Expands the ego. Thankfully, another by-product of meditation is that if we're masking a problem, we become more likely to see it, as Zen expands our awareness. Zen cultivates a Witness perspective where we're able to *be* awareness, see ourselves in situations, and choose our responses, rather than be caught up in knee-jerk reactions. I started seeing the game I was playing at NASA, hell-bent in my pursuit of being an astronaut. I could see how I was using my training as a way to be more perfect in the eyes of others, trying to say the right thing and do the right thing so that I might impress the right people, and NASA might give me my dream. When things like my heart wouldn't get with the program, I'd try to center myself more deeply. I knew something was off in this approach, but it just felt so *necessary* at the time. I'd like to say expanded awareness eventually broke through my delusion, but it was helped along at 3:27 one morning by that pesky heart racing over 200 beats per minute and sending pain down my left arm. *I'm thirty-four years old*, I thought, *having what for all the world feels like a heart attack.* That woke me up.

As our awareness expands, we may face uncomfortable truths, but things generally get better. We're more effective and better able to resonate with others. Expanded awareness is good for our careers, good for other people, and good for our life generally. This is the mainstream, business case stage of Zen (and other forms of meditation), where we can use Zen to create even greater value in our work. But two forces start competing at this stage. One is the force of complacency. Because things are improving, maybe they're good enough, and we don't have to do anything more. But the other force has alluring possibility: we start catching glimpses of "something more," beyond our ego, and we're drawn to the next stage.

Challenges the ego. Stop here in the taming process if you're interested only in the conventional value of Zen. Or, press on if you can't help yourself. For this next stage sneaks up on us, but starts moving us away from conventional notions of value. We may have gotten into Zen training for perfectly sound reasons we could explain to anyone. But soon we start catching glimpses of a radically different sense of self, much bigger than this skin, and not really a corpuscular "self" at all. We see a whirl of leaves whipped up by an eddy of wind and it stirs something in us, reminds us. We catch a glimpse of our own nature: absolute emptiness, whipped into temporary form, held in place by the causes and conditions we call a lifetime.

Never mind, the ego assures us. *Move along, nothing to see here.* And we go back to our daily routine, our familiar work, not realizing—yet—that these familiar habits are part of the causes and conditions holding our ego in place. If we dare mention this glimpse to a co-worker, friend or family member, unless they've already been down this road they're likely to pull us back into the familiar, maybe with a fear-tinged comment like, "Oh, don't start going off the deep end on me."

Then another glimpse: *Dammit, what was that?* We're filled with a sense of awe and oneness, even as our ego is challenged by what it has seen. At first, the ego tries to give these glimpses meaning, often taking credit. If we've grown up in a monotheistic culture, we might say, *Why, I'm having a mystical experience of feeling one-with God. I must be blessed to have such an insight.* Or training in Zen, our ego might take credit this way: *My sitting is so strong, I'm now able to see my true nature, like they always talk about in Zen. I've truly arrived.*

The deeper truth is that this is simply our ego, challenged at is coreless core, trying to arouse enough complacency to keep its own game going. Because something in it knows that if we honor these glimpses, not as accomplishments *of* the self, but as a truth *about* our self, the game as we've known it will be turned upside down. Were it not for the accompanying awe of these glimpses, we might be able to ignore them. But if they keep happening, they're likely to stir our innate longing to be whole. In truth, this longing has been driving our development all along. It has been working in us since we formed the very ego that separated us as individual humans in the first place. Catching these glimpses, we can't go back to forgetting we saw them. We have to go forward.

Assaults the ego. At some point, I just had to dive in. As I shared earlier, it happened when my life thoroughly fell apart and I quit protecting its contours. I wish I could tell you that the decision was made once and for all and that things got easier from there, but that's not true. I would dive into *sesshin*, have some mind-blowing experience—a whopping glimpse of my no-self nature—but then come back to the habits of my daily work life and a familiar "self" would return, while all that bigness faded to memory. It would drive me crazy. I changed my diet to mostly vegetables so my body would get more flexible and I could sit better. I changed my morning routine so I could sit longer. I changed where I lived—divorce will do that—and moved into an apartment over the dojo. But still, I was occasionally diving in and then retreating to the safe shore of a familiar life. I felt like a confused, awkward hypocrite: going to work every day, now in a senior role on the Space Station Program, keeping it together on the surface, even continuing to teach Aikido and Zen like I knew what I was doing. Yet underneath, I was nothing but dry rot.

I started writing more. Listening more. And learning more. Intermingled with all the confusion were streams of clarity. Sitting stabilized me. Meditation and *hara* breathing helped me manage my own stress going through this process. I've heard sitting at this stage aptly described as creating a safe chamber for the internal combustion of the ego. NASA was also good enough to send me to a series of leadership development programs intended to prepare me for Senior Executive Service in the government. Instead, these programs started stirring a deep passion, an extension of the teaching I'd been doing at the dojo for years, and a whole new direction for my life. I wanted to learn everything I could about leadership, coaching, and professional development. And I kept writing.

I've seen and heard similar stories unfold in the lives of many of my Zen-training colleagues: they dive in, and their life changes. The body starts changing and asks for changes in one's life. Tenuous relationships end and new ones grow. Work shifts in its focus. As we start to vibrate in a new way, it's as if the antenna that we are starts picking up new frequencies. I'm often asked by people whether it's possible to have a career and train deeply in Zen. And my answer is, "Sure, just don't expect anything to stay the same." Or put another way, anything you're gripping onto, determined to keep the same, will become a sticking point. The ego gloms onto virtually anything for self-definition: stuff, relationships, title, résumé, roles, morning rituals, political orientation, favorite foods and on and on. What we learn at this stage is that none of that really defines us—unless we insist upon it at all cost, at which point it becomes a prison bar of our own making. The more prison bars we insist upon, the smaller our prison. The happier option is finding we can let go, let go, let go—and life keeps getting bigger.

The other truth of this stage of assault is that we can't navigate it alone. Hopefully we're already working with a teacher we trust, but if we haven't found one yet, we need to find one now. While it's easy to look back on this time and make sense of it, it doesn't make sense at the time. Rather, our sense-making apparatus is exactly what's getting assaulted, deconstructed, and is not a trustworthy guide through this patch of forest. One needs a trustworthy teacher. It is said when the student is ready the teacher appears. How boundlessly grateful I am for that tidy fact.

Reframes the ego. At some point, everything empties. The world flips around. And rather than looking at the world from the perspective of a solid object, you suddenly see you're nothing more than a temporary product of its temporary conditions, even as you are the forces that shaped those conditions: the creative power of the universe with hands and feet. And this temporary form—complex as it is—has also whipped up an ego that you get to play this round of life with. This very ego that had felt like such an enemy to be conquered is now a tool in your hands. How do you want to use it?

Reorganizes the ego. An "aha" awakening is not an end, but a new beginning, as the real work begins to re-organize around this new insight. This is not unlike learning in general: we may have an "aha" realization that we have to change our career, for example, but then the real work starts in realigning our daily activities to manifest that insight. But all of this gets supercharged when the bottom falls out of the self altogether. In a physical sense, this bottoming out is a deep relaxation in the body that supports freer vibration and greater agility. Once the ego is re-framed as a tool to be used in service of life, everything looks different. Everything is open to being re-thought, reworked, re-invented. This stage resembles the assault stage in terms of the letting go that keeps opening us to a fuller expression of ourselves. But it doesn't have the same level of fear, because fear can only hide out in a self that needs protection.

The challenge of this stage is, one again, complacency. In some ways, it's an even greater risk than before because we've had some realization. "Are you going to be satisfied with that shabby enlightenment?" we read in the Zen literature, the scolding of a Zen master to a student, a good reminder at this stage. For we may have experienced our empty nature and can talk about it at length, but do we function from it moment by moment? It comes to a question of: How high are our standards? One of the things any of us who knew Tanouye Roshi would say we admired in him was that he showed us, through his own living example, how high standards could be. He embodied a depth of all-in training, what the Japanese call *shugyo*. Tanouye realized that we didn't need more people who just had an "aha" experience, but rather more people who could function from that freedom. It was his mission to bring not just Zen, but also this standard of training—*shugyo*—to the West.

Life itself can also teach us, as challenging conditions and people trigger us and we find ourselves stuck on the rocks of a deep insecurity, a debilitating illness, an irrecoverable loss. We'll find places where we know the right thing to do, but we still can't do it; where our walk and our talk don't match, giving us more opportunity to work out the glitches. In Rinzai Zen, stages of koan training beyond one's initial awakening guide this re-organization: they catalyze a re-conception of the world as we know it and find our sticking points. But the real koan we're solving is our own life: we're realizing how to function with our particular skills from absolute emptiness.

What this stage opened up for me was an expansive purposefulness to work. In earlier days, I had worked to prove myself. Now, at this new stage, everything flipped around and my work became a way to focus my energy in service of others. It radically changed my listening—opened up my antennae—because my reference point had become: what's needed? Nothing to prove and no one needing proving.

Uses the ego. Getting out of our own way—at last!—we are free to create according to the universal energy that resonates through our differentiated gifts. As Lao Tzu would say, in non-doing (i.e., non-assertion of the ego), we do everything. This is the *wu-wei*—effortless effort—that perhaps intrigued us about this Way from the start. Birds aren't clumsy. Waves don't doubt themselves. Mountains aren't afraid. But clumsiness, doubt and fear pervade the world of human beings. Humans, of course, are more complex than birds, waves and mountains, so all the more wondrous when a complex human being can function as freely as a bird finding air currents, as naturally as nature itself. It brings the possibility of re-unification directly into our human experience, which resonates with the deepest chord of truth in all beings. *Myo* is the word for it in Japanese: *wondrous.* It is work that gives life.

Such work inspires or gives fearlessness to others because it comes from a place of inspiration and fearlessness. Just as a stone rubbing manifests the contours of the stone it came from, so the work of emptiness shows emptiness. Others may not be able to explain why they feel better being with a certain person, why a certain speech inspires them, or a certain design moves them, yet work that gives life has this effect on people. It is the most universally resonant signal we can share, because it stirs a truth in all beings. Imagine a world with a critical mass of people who function from this connectedness and give life to what they do! Imagine your world this free.

Only you can decide how far you want to drive this process in your own life. But however far you take it, you now have the tools to tame a mind too small and a body too tight for what you're determined to grow into. Better integrated, tuned and tamed, what can you now resonate into being? What becomes possible? Prepare to be surprised as we turn to the potentially wondrous applications of resonance in Part III.

RESONANCE RECAP—TAME

- "Sit twenty minutes a day and it will change your life."
- The unflinching stillness of *Zazen* tames impulses, quiets the runaway mind, and builds the condition for facing into fears.
- Expanding beyond our egocentric nature expands our resonance with others and widens our range of sensitivity to universal energy.
- Taming the ego happens in stages, and pivots at a point where we see through the ego altogether.
- If we keep deepening our practice and reorganize around our no-self nature, we increasingly resonate with what is universal in all beings, and our work gives life.

PART III

USE RESONANCE TO MAKE A DIFFERENCE

Whereby you apply yourself as an instrument of the Way

6

RELATIONSHIPS

I was frightened by Tanouye Roshi. I wanted so much for him to like me, be impressed by me. And instead, he would slice and dice me up into little pieces, reduce me to tears, make me feel like a total failure. In other words, he was an outstanding teacher. But his frequent irritation with me was also genuine. I remember one morning in particular when the vibe between us was very bad. He was angry at me for something—I don't recall the specifics—but I do recall that I was certain I was right and he had misunderstood the whole situation. I was meditating in the dojo, he was in the adjoining kitchen, but even at a distance I could feel his anger, while the little voice in my head kept repeating its side of the story, again and again. At some point it quieted, and an expansive state opened up. I could suddenly feel the whole picture, what it felt like to be Tanouye when the disruption named Ginny blew into town. I could feel what a clumsy pain in the ass I had been. Filled with clarity and remorse, after the meditation session ended, I marched into the kitchen and poured out my heartfelt apology to Tanouye. He nodded, offered me a cup of tea. Our relationship strengthened from that day onward.

Since that pivotal morning, I've had the experience countless times of seeing how changes in me shift the relationships I'm engaged in. If the relationship has been stuck or troubled, when I free up, it frees up. If the relationship has been skating the surface of an issue, when I deepen my listening, it deepens. I bet you could find similar examples in your own life, and I draw your attention to them because it is through the relationships of our life that our application of resonance is most direct, up-close and personal. We don't change other people except through resonance. Which means we change ourselves first.

Applying resonance to the relationships of our life is powerful and wide-ranging. In a sense, life is nothing but a stream of relationships between you and the world, from people to situations, each with an energetic quality affected by how you engage them. In the next chapter we'll see how the same principles of resonance apply to situations, but in this chapter, we focus on resonance in human relationships, and how we can tune in to the energy of others to build love, take away fear, reduce conflict, or spread our influence.

We have particular power to apply resonance in human relationships because we are, well, human. Because all things vibrate and change according to their nature, we are better able to send and receive resonant signals with another human than we are to move a mountain or communicate with a moth. Some people are closer to lard-ass largo while others are springy allegro, but we all live and breathe, walk, talk and chew gum in a recognizable range of human frequencies. That means we can use ourselves as sensitive receivers and powerful transmitters to meet others where they are, and to get them moving with us and us with them.

We also have a particular need to affect human relationships because we couldn't exist without them. Every child is conceived in relationship, born in relationship, and only makes it through infancy in relationship. The most basic human needs, from food and shelter to love and belonging, are only met through relationships, and only met well through loving relationships. But what exactly does it mean for a relationship to be loving from a resonance perspective, and how can we apply our more resonant self to building relationships that are more loving? Let's go there.

BE LOVE

Physics doesn't use the word "love," but it does talk a great deal about attraction. Every chunk of matter, for example, attracts every other in proportion to its mass. The big, heavy earth exerts such a powerful attractive force we give it a name: gravity. How we relate to gravity shows up in our physical body and in the way we literally carry our life experience. We can have the "weight of the world" on our shoulders, as in the collapsed postures of huddled masses. Or we can stand tall and upright in gravity and feel the lift of alignment through our spine, something we return to with every breath in Zen training. When we can align with a larger force like gravity, rather than fight with it, our subjective experience is one of joy. We feel bigger, stronger, more of who we are.

This same principle applies in our relationships with people and fostering the subjective experience we call love. Every interaction you have with a person has an energetic quality or "vibe." You're part of that field and so are they. How you relate to that energy shows up in your physical body. For example, if they smile, we could start to measure neurons in you that light up and likely create a smile on your lips. When they start talking, we could strap an EEG device on your head and see how the communication is changing your brainwaves. When they touch your skin, we could see the vibration of nerve cells triggering the release of hormones into your bloodstream. But those are just the objective measures. Subjectively, what you experience is a positive, neutral or negative quality to the relationship. You engage it a certain way—just as you engage gravity a certain way—and if your two energies align, rather than fight with each other, your subjective experience is one of joy. You feel amplified, stronger, more of who you are.

So, to paraphrase Eckhart Tolle, while we commonly say, "I love you," what we're really saying is "I love how I feel in your presence." Or, "I love how you make me feel about me." That's not saying we don't care about the other person. Indeed, we may find great joy in doing things that increase the other's joy, and as their increased joy pours into our shared field, our joy increases further still. I would submit that this amplification of joy mirrored in one another, like the mirrors of a laser, leads to the phase shift we experience as falling in love or the deepest, loving relationships of our life.

As a Zen priest, I'm sometimes asked to officiate the marriage of a couple and, while I don't have a formal premarital counseling routine, a question I often ask each person is: Do you care more about the other person's happiness than your own? Of course, in that context, most people say "yes." But the energy of that "yes" on the scale of *obligatory* to *resounding* is a darn good predictor of the success of that relationship. An obligatory "yes" is saying, "I love how you make me feel about me, and if you don't make me feel good about me, we're going to have trouble." If both give a resounding "yes," they're saying, "I love how you make me feel, and I'm at my happiest when you're happy, so I will adjust to support your greatest happiness." In the first case, you get a relationship that works in good times. In the second case, you get laser-like, superconducting love.

What's true for the most loving relationships of our life is true for our relationships in general: they become more loving when we, ourselves, are more loving. And the two qualities that make us loving are connection and positive intent. Connection is empathy; it is feeling one-with another. It is allowing my subjective experience to be changed by you, indeed, experiencing you and me as one dynamic; you are a part of me and I am a part of you. Connection is like potential energy or voltage; it creates the condition in which a great deal of energy can flow.

Positive intent is the current, or the energy that flows. If I really want what's best for you, the energy-directing process we call *mind* starts pouring energy across our connection. The connection gives me feedback— *Is my energy is a hit or a miss?*— and because my positive intent is determined to make it a hit, my energy keeps adjusting until it aligns with yours, getting our signals to add up. Much of this, of course, passes beneath our consciousness. At the surface of our conversation, it might show up as me asking about your interests, matching your rate of breathing and speaking, and listening for where the conversation needs to go because when you start getting excited about something, that excitement registers in me as well. This is not a rare or exotic skill and is entirely trainable. Indeed, it's used by parents, professional coaches, and counselors every day. If we were to measure what's happening energetically in one of these connected, loving conversations, we'd see signals adding up and amplifying one another. No wonder we feel bigger and like more of who we are in a field of love. We *are*.

The best piece of coaching advice I ever heard applies to building loving relationships in general, and it came from that turned-around relationship with Tanouye Roshi: "Become the other, go from there." "Become the other" is the connection. It's not connection like boxcars on a train are connected. Rather, it's connection like interpenetrating waves of empathetic vibration. I feel your subjective experience inasmuch as I allow it to change my own. The *Connection* practices (see box) offer several ways to melt into this experience of one-withness. Experiencing this expanded we-space, we "go from there" with positive intent, which opens us to an expanded sense of self. When we build relationships this way, we are love.

But wait, you may be thinking, *aren't there dangers to letting someone in this much? Don't we have to protect ourselves from bad actors with bad energy? What happens if I'm trying to be one-with and the other person wants nothing of it?* And so we come face-to-face with what gets in the way of building loving relationships, and that is—fear.

CONNECTION

To become the other, we start with an inner relaxation and deep listening. We might imagine our entire body becoming an eardrum that's ready to receive what even the most subtle signals will register.

To become the other is to get on their same wavelength. We can subtly look and feel for what frequencies they're expressing and initially match them. For example:

- **Walking**—if you're walking together, match step. Feel into how to make your conversation fall in with the rhythm of the walking.

- **Breathing**—Feel into how they're breathing, which you might sense in their subtle physical movements or their pace of talking. Match and steady their breathing with your own, either one-for-one or by making your breath a slower multiple of theirs, sending your breath deep into your *hara*.

- **Talking**—Listen for their cadence of speech and the emotional, energetic quality of it. Match the energy.

- **Moving**—Even if you're not walking, watch for and feel the cadence of their physical movement and gestures. Are they slow and lumbering or fast and frenetic? If they were a musical instrument in an orchestra, would they be more like a timpani drum or a piccolo?

- **Conversational content**—Sense where they are, what they care about, what frame of mind they're in. Feel it and start there.

How we "go from there" will depend on circumstances; we might slow them down, or we might hang out where they are and let them inform our intuition. However we proceed, we'll want to keep this visceral listening active to stay connected and sense whether resonance is building.

TAKE AWAY FEAR

Kristi is a physician. She's one of many who have come through our IZL program tailored to those in healthcare, called HEAL, which is how I got to know her. So many healthcare practitioners are trained to "put up shields" and protect themselves from the downtrodden, difficult, and damaged lives of some of their patients. And yet those shields can also lead to burnout, disengagement, and days filled with chart-ticking transactions. It is like shuttering a house to keep the wind and sun from pouring in; we can do it, but after a while, the house becomes suffocating. When we unplug from the energy around us, it is like running on battery power. Again, we can do it, but after a while, we'll run out of steam.

There is another way, which is to be one-with the suffering of another and let it drop cleanly through oneself, without hooks. Embodying this quality is something we train for in Zen and the HEAL program, using the very practices you saw in Part II. This is what Kristi embodied as she faced the door of a patient, Brad, who she knew was in great pain and deep trouble. He was a self-employed contractor with severe back pain which made it impossible for him to work. Yet this work was all he knew; his grandfather had taught him the trade and he had never done anything else. He couldn't afford treatments for his back pain because he couldn't work, and he couldn't work because of the pain. Kristi knew Brad felt hopeless and angry at the world, and at her as well; if only she had ordered the MRI when he first asked for it, he would have met his deductible. All of this flashed through Kristi's mind as she stood at the door Brad was impatiently waiting behind.

Kristi was at a loss, feeling stuck, in what we call coping mode. In the past, she might have just given him a prescription and a referral for physical therapy—anything to get out of the room quickly. But she remembered from her HEAL training how to deal with coping mode: relax, enter and add value. She dropped her breath into *hara*, and opened not only the door, but herself, remaining honest and curious as she engaged Brad. As she put it, "We joined. He shifted. I listened and asked unlikely questions for a doctor-patient visit. He came out of the visit with new, completely unexpected plans to teach his craft to others, and wanting to have coffee with me to discuss his ideas." Brad is now out of pain and doesn't need to see Kristi anymore.

What Kristi cured in Brad was not his back pain, but his isolating fear. In a cycle even more vicious than Brad's work dilemma, fear grows in the cracks where we feel separate and alone, and then makes us feel even more separate, more alone, which builds more fear, fueling all of its coping-mode manifestations: anger, depression, denial, defensiveness, and blame. Vicious as it is, this cycle is no accident. As we saw in Chapter 2, it's exactly how our mind-body amplifies a signal through resonance. The body has a pain, which triggers a thought, *I can't work, I'm screwed*, and that triggers an emotion—despair!—that floods the body with chemicals, which in turn sends distress signals back to the brain saying, in effect, "Send me more thoughts that match this desperate feeling."

By joining one-with Brad, Kristi interrupted the cycle. Fear could not grow in the connection she established, and her openness and curiosity drew out new possibilities in Brad's thinking. In Zen, we call this taking away fear, and it's considered to be the highest art form in any profession. But notice, it's not a thought-based rationalizing with the fear or even an effort to "fix." Kristi knew there was no quick fix and was not saying, "There, there, nothing to worry about. Your back will heal someday. . . ." No. As she said: "We joined. He shifted." To take away fear is to create connection which interrupts the delusion of separateness where fear otherwise grows.

Translate this to your own life and, if your experience matches mine, you'll see countless opportunities to do this. The classic Venus-Mars exchange comes to mind where a woman pours out her story of a struggle to her husband, and he counters with all kinds of rational remedies, she gets more exasperated, he becomes more rational, and finally she blurts out, "I don't want your solution, I want you to hear me!" How often do we replace genuine connection with efforts to fix and figure things out for other people? I know as a coach and teacher, I have been guilty of this countless times. And yet, as I find now, the more I simply connect with people with positive intent and curiosity, the more they find their own solutions. Or even spookier, the more they come up with things I thought, but did not say (something that is particularly welcome when it comes to influence).

Moreover, this is not an exhausting way to work. Rather, it's rejuvenating, as it continually re-amplifies the truth of our connected being over the delusion of separateness. As Kristi told me later, "Doctoring in this way feels like I'm using good form as I am more effective and sustainable. I'm not exhausted at the end of the day. I used to think that being a doctor legitimized my compassion; now I feel that Zen has legitimized my doctoring."

REDUCE CONFLICT

What would the exchange with Brad have been like if he hadn't been open to joining with Kristi? Surely there are people in our lives who are so conflicted—so caught up in their fears and inner loops—that establishing a connection and taking away fear seems impossible. This is especially true if our own positive intent toward them is challenged, say, if they've caused us great harm or worry, and we're angry as all get-out. How can resonance serve or guide us in even the most conflicted relationships of our life? We can't eliminate interpersonal conflict, because conflict is built into what it is to be human. But we can productively work with conflict, starting with our own.

I recall from my days on the Aikido mat, being attacked by all kinds of people with all kinds of energy. Some were people I loved to work with because they followed energy so easily: they were flexible, almost buoyant, and would embrace the fall I would throw them into with the vigor of a gymnast on a dismount. Others were like lead. I would get exasperated working with these tense, resisting creatures, until I realized that my attitude was making *me* tense and resistive, too. What I learned, over time, was that the more tense and resistive the other person was, the more relaxed and centered I had to be. No surprise that these are among the basic principles of Aikido—posted right there in black and white at the front of the dojo, starting with "relax completely." I understood the principles conceptually from the start, but could only truly embody them after years of practice. Over those years, the range of people I could joyfully work with expanded, until virtually no one exasperated me. Or, put another way, I got out of my own way until there was no "me" to get exasperated.

Aikido, which translates as "the Way of harmonizing energy" is itself a practice in resonance, i.e., getting energy to add up in new ways. But how do we harmonize with someone who has just attacked us, either physically or psychologically? While you may think physical and psychological attacks are different, they register similarly in our nervous system, and have common roots in our sense of who we are. Those roots, as we've seen, relate to having a human set of needs that may not get met, from physical needs to security to self-actualization. Those roots may also relate to the violation of values that feel core to our identity, such as fairness, justice, goodness or beauty. When we get triggered, something about our ego's sense of self is at stake, and the more unconscious the fear, the more it sucks us in, making mountains out of molehills. A driver cuts us off on the freeway, and we're enraged. A boss doesn't appreciate us, and we totally disengage. Our spouse says we look fat in those jeans, and it's an existential crisis.

While the techniques to handle physical attacks may differ from those for psychological attacks, we can use the same principles, starting with "relax completely." This deceptively simple sounding principle runs far deeper than shaking out the superficial tension in our shoulders or taking a casual attitude. It's owning our own stuff and not getting stuck there, seeing our triggers and being able to breathe through them to a relaxed state. The fact is, when we're triggered, we're not relaxed completely—duh! Something in us is tense and separate, which we may resonate into the person who triggered us who then gets further amped up themselves. Conversely, if we have the Aikido-trained reaction—namely, the more tense and triggered the other person is, the more relaxed we become—we can de-escalate conflict with a broader range of people.

Like Aikido, this takes practice. Conceptually you can understand this principle in a few seconds. But to live it is the work of years. In Aikido, we can practice by repeating physical techniques again and again, but what can we practice to reduce conflict in the relationships of our lives? First, we can practice seeing more deeply into our own triggers and fears using the *Taming Fear* practice in Chapter 5. We can take this a step further using the framework of the energy patterns and the fears and triggers characteristic of each pattern. These are summarized in Table 6-1; see where you recognize yourself. Reflecting on a conflicted relationship in your life, see where you recognize the other person.

We can further reframe such conflicted relationships by considering them not as annoyances, but as teachers. Start by affirming that you can reduce conflict in any relationship, and then notice in yourself if any counter examples arise—like, what about those really hard cases? What about that jerk who gossips about me to others? Or that conniving asshole who has been so cruel? Right there we find the points of practice, because right there is where we get stuck to a self having a problem. That's where our mind stops. So, what do we have to do "in here" to relax our mind and body, to re-enter the stream of universal energy?

Table 6-1. Conflict across the Four Energy Patterns

	DRIVER	ORGANIZER	COLLABORATOR	VISIONARY
Causes of conflict: (Triggers)	Losing power or face, not winning; not achieving the target Faults in others (too slow, incompetent) Things not happening fast enough	Being wrong or improper; not getting it right Being rushed or pushed around, abrasiveness Unethical, unjust situations Being ridiculed, not being recognized or appreciated	Rejection, being left out, ignored, out of the spotlight Lack of teamwork or loyalty Having authority or credibility questioned Not having enough fun or variety	Conflict itself, hostility, lack of harmony, lack of fairness Routine, being hemmed in or pinned down on details; no chance to be imaginative or spontaneous Lack of risk or adventure
Deep fears	Not powerful or strong enough, not achieving enough, not safe	Not good or smart enough, not worthy, not able to right a wrong	Not loved or liked enough, not beautiful, not in the tribe	Not authentic or self-actualized enough, not free, not connected
Typical reactions to conflict:	Pushes harder Gets abrasive, abusive; runs over people	Explains, justifies, repeats their logic Freezes, gets quiet, stuck, withdrawn	Gets overly dramatic, loud, digs in heels Personally attacks; teases, mocks	Goes away, wanders around Emotionally withdraws, even if still physically present
What one needs to move forward	A way to save face and win at something Restored honor, strength	A way to feel good about oneself again, a way to be right Recognition, appreciation	A way to get involved or interacting again Re-engagement	A way to re-establish fairness, get things flowing again Restored harmony

The *Trigger-proofing* exercise (see box) takes you through a practice for doing this. What you'll find is that the cusp between coping and co-creating, between being locked in conflict and being free, is always the same and is always *acceptance*. Acceptance doesn't mean we like somebody or something, it means we take it as it is. It doesn't mean we do nothing and let people walk all over us. It does mean we act as the whole picture, connected one-with-the-other as an aspect of our whole Self. Far from being ineffective, this is our most effective state, which is why the most successful Samurai of old were attracted to Zen. It allowed them to transcend a separate ego-self and operate as a force of nature.

If you were to physically model a state of acceptance right now, as if you were acting it out in a game of charades—try it—you'd instantly feel an inner shift toward relaxation. Physically as we relax, we vibrate more freely with what's going on around us—i.e. universal energy. As we get tense, we physically shut down the vibration in parts of our self, which sends its own energetic signal of separation. If "I" am separate from "you," fear has a chance to grow and conflict to escalate. If I'm completely relaxed and accepting of you exactly in your conflicted state—a cut-off and frightened aspect of the whole Self that I am—I can intuitively act in the most capable way. And how do we get the hang of seeing conflicted others as frightened, cut-off aspects of ourselves? By continually seeing and opening to the frightened, cut-off aspects *in* ourselves—i.e., our triggers and fears.

As the *Trigger-proofing* exercise suggests, you do well to closely examine a conflicted relationship in your life for how it triggers you. Ask: What you're afraid may be true about you, and see if you can accept even *that* and still find your power. Repeat this practice again and again, and you'll be developing a deep compassion for how triggers work, how common they are, how they're always based in fear, how even triggers that you want to change in yourself don't change overnight, and neither can other people's. And yet, the more consciously you work with triggers, the freer you are from their grip, the wider the range of people you can harmonize with, and the more you can resonate the same freedom in others.

Un-trapped by triggers, you just might be able to help someone in conflict move out of it. But truthfully, that's a bonus; people change in accordance with their own nature, not in accordance with your desire to change them. And if they change because of the exchange with you, it's because you changed first and they were able to resonate with a new possibility. The last row of Table 6-1 can give you a sense of what people, triggered in the different patterns, need to move forward. But your own insight from working your own triggers and establishing a genuine connection in the moment, just as Kristi did, create the best context for the right words and actions to emerge.

Since conflict is one of the great generative forces and, even when we don't want it, is here to stay, how fortunate that we can learn how to use it.

TRIGGER-PROOFING

The upside of conflicted relationships is that they give us a chance to work our triggers. We can't free ourselves from triggers we don't face. So, in a way, people who push our buttons do us a great service. That is, if we're willing to do the trigger-proofing work. Here's how.

- Think of a person with whom you've had conflict, or are in conflict now, and write their name. Picture them clearly.

- Describe how they trigger you; what do they say or do?

- Trace the root of that trigger to its deeper fear by asking: So what? Why does that trouble me? And then what? Ultimately: What do I fear may be true about me? Refer to Figure 5-4 to answer: what need are you afraid won't be met enough? In what sense might *you* not be enough?

(cont.)

- Put that piece of paper on the floor and stand on it. Odd as this may seem, you want to physically feel what it means to own this fear, totally accept it's a fear operating in you AND you are much bigger than it. Standing on this fear, what is within your power to do?

- Write down what you can do in this relationship, regardless of what the other person does. What is your power to act? What can you learn?

SPREAD INFLUENCE

I was working with a group in a Zen Leader program, and we had just finished an influence activity, riffing off Tanouye Roshi's adage: "Become the other, go from there." Once we were clear about what we wanted from a particular person, we "became" that person by physically standing, moving, and making gestures that person would make, even as we imagined our actual self approaching them with our proposition. I had reviewed with the group how influence works: when the other person perceives that what we want them to do, or what we're willing to exchange, aligns with their interests, then they resonate with it. "Wow," said Alex as he opened our debrief, "I thought I knew this person well. But as soon as I started moving as them and imagined me and my idea, I could feel their resistance and what they're afraid of. No wonder I haven't been getting through."

Such is the power of getting down to the physical level when we're trying to get someone moving with us. From Dale Carnegie's 1930s classic, *How to Win Friends and Influence People,* to the stages of emotional intelligence, to countless books written on marketing, sales and objection handling, there's no shortage of tips and techniques for influencing. But it's at the physical level that we sense whether any of them are actually working. When energy builds in an influencing conversation—when there's engaged dialogue, excitement, head nodding, bright eyes, ideas building on one another—resonance is happening. When resistance builds—when there's heaviness, effort, distracted eyes, uncomfortable lulls in conversation—resonance is not happening. It's pretty simple.

Simple, but not always easy to know what to do. Rather than start with technique, we do well to look to the underlying energy and the ground we've already covered to discover conditions favorable to influence.

- **Be Love:** Be sincerely *for* the person you want to influence. Check in with yourself and be totally honest. If you're not truly wanting to serve this person's interests, why should they follow you? If you are serving their interests, how can you show it?

- **Take Away Fear:** Be connected, one-with this person and one-with the energy around you. If you're a separate self trying to "sell" something, fear can grow in the crack between the two of you. Eliminate the crack.

- **Reduce Conflict:** Relax completely and don't let their resistance trigger you. This may be the day they see that what you want them to do is exactly right for them, or it may not be. Let connected intuition be your guide, not fear-based pushing.

If we take to influence as a separate "I"—selling something to a separate "you"—we're already sub-optimizing the exchange. Yes, influence brings to our relationships an intention, a direction we want the other person or people to move toward. It may be largely in our interest and only slightly in their interest, or it may be in our shared interest, but they don't see it yet. The fact is, we're asking for a change in them—something they have to let go of, or do differently, to get moving with us. How willing are we to be changed in that exchange to get in sync with them? If we're relaxed, connected and flexible, we naturally go where things go and we, too, are changed. If we're fixed and expect all the change to be on their side, it may never work. It's pure physics: two vibrating systems can sync up more quickly when both can flex in their vibrational frequency. If only one can change and the other is fixed, resonating together will certainly take longer, and may never happen.

So, the more we enter influencing conversations with connection *and* curiosity for how our idea can work for or be amplified through others, the more we, and maybe even our idea, are changed, and the more likely we'll generate resonance. That said, much has also been studied and written about the effectiveness of different influencing approaches, and it can be helpful to know the range of ways to make an ask, and reasons why a person may agree, from painting an inspiring picture of the future to agreeing to a personal favor. The energy patterns are again a useful guide for which of these techniques are most likely to catch resonance with a person or situation, as summarized in Table 6-2. Yet the relative importance of connected energy over technique cannot be overstated. If a strong connection is present, even if we stumble over our words or are sloppy in our technique, our positive intent will come through. Conversely, without a connection, no matter how polished our technique or proper the outcome, it always leaves a bad taste. And it should, because we're using people, not serving them.

Table 6-2. Influencing Approaches across the Energy Patterns

	DRIVER	ORGANIZER	COLLABORATOR	VISIONARY
Effective ways to influence	Show how it's a win for them, how it beats the competition, or changes the game.	Show how it's right by a higher standard, rights a wrong, puts an issue to rest, is more efficient, or gets stuff done.	Show how it's good for people, helps customers, is more fun or sustainable.	Show how it serves a worthy purpose, realizes a vision, serves future generations, or inspires greatness.
	Show how it helps them reach their goals, raise the bar.	Show how it helps them, be responsible, take ownership, and do the right thing.	Show how it makes them more visible, and core to the tribe.	Show how it restores fairness or harmony.
	Also: Get to the point, don't waste their time; be clear about your ask, align with their goals.	Also: Let them think about it. Invite their questions; let them voice their doubts.	Also: Let them play with the idea; ask as a favor, and "owe" them one; enlist other strong relationships to support your case.	Also: Invite their imagination, let them wander with the idea so they can connect dots, allow divergence before convergence.

Up to this point, we've talked about spreading influence from you outward, which is the conventional way of thinking about it: "I" have an idea or something I want from you and, even without position power, I'm able to influence you so I can get it. That's no small skill, and no wonder teaching it has been a part of leadership programs in the more than twenty-five years I've been in the field. But it's still backwards thinking and way too small. For how did "I" come up with the idea? Our ego likes to think it just made it up all on its own, but that's not how things work. Energy, including thought energy, is not created or destroyed. It's transferred and re-formed through resonance. Thoughts and ideas come from stimulation, which can be overt stimulation through the senses, or something more subtle like picking up a trend in the Zeitgeist, sensing what's ready to happen, or resonating with the flow of universal energy and letting it change us one inspiration after another.

That's not to say the ego self plays no role. As we saw in Part II, our ego has to be a willing participant in how sensitively we tune ourselves to the energy around us. But it's an especially useful point to remember when it comes to influence that the best and biggest ideas we might want to influence people around are not purely "our" ideas. They are ideas that found us. We might be among the early adopters to vibrate with them, and we can amplify those signals in the Zeitgeist through our influencing. But if the idea is in some sense ripe to happen, others will resonate with it as well. Indeed, a good sign that an idea is ready to happen is when we can feel the expansiveness of no one selling and no one being sold to. I hope you can feel yourself relax into the bigness of this truth: influence at its best is connecting people to the same Way that inspired us.

Which moves us squarely into the realm of leadership. We turn that that next.

RESONANCE RECAP—RELATIONSHIPS

- Be love: Become the other and be for the other as an aspect of your whole Self.
- Take away fear: Fear can only grow in the crack of separateness and, regardless of what you can do for the matter at hand, you can always seal the crack through your own connectedness.
- Reduce Conflict: Let conflict be your opportunity to free up your own triggers.
- Influence works best when it connects people to the same universal energy that inspired us; no one selling and no one sold to.

7

LEADERSHIP

My early fears that Zen would change my life were spot on, yet when it came, the change was more freeing than fearful. As a leader at NASA, having been launched into management, not space, I led the integration of the parts and pieces that would become the International Space Station. It was not going well. We were re-designing faster than we could agree on what we were building, meaning issues piled up faster than we could resolve them, tempers frayed, voices rose, and people were getting exhausted.

Meanwhile, at night I was running a dojo teaching Aikido and Zen. Here I watched people become more resilient, centered, and able to work well in tense situations. It started gnawing on me: this deep, physical training of the dojo could be of enormous help in the workplace. As I was fortunate to take part in NASA's leadership development programs, I met world-class teachers of leadership, yet no one was integrating mind and body. Something in me knew this was my work, and that signal grew over the next two years through my inner alignment and outer synchronicities. I saved money, learned everything I could about leadership and teams, applied it to the best contribution I made to NASA and—you can't make this stuff up—fell in love with and later married one of those world-class teachers and started a leadership development company.

So what was the difference between my astronaut dream that died on the vine, and realizing my dream of teaching a new way of leadership development? Resonance. The first one did not match me and the conditions, and the second one did. While it may seem like circular logic to claim this in hindsight, even along the way there are surefire signs of energy building—or not—around a goal or dream. In this chapter, we explore how to build and listen for resonance in realizing your goals and dreams, which is what we mean by leadership. We go back to the swingset of your youth, and how you learned the principle of "driving rhythm," pumping your legs at just the right moment, and feeling the joy of the swing going higher. Through examples of resonance at work, you'll learn that not all systems are as immediately gratifying as a swing, but also how to sense the rate at which people and systems *can* respond, which is "resonance hunting" on the human scale. You'll learn how to distinguish necessary perseverance from useless stubbornness, and how you're able to catalyze more change the more you let life change you.

WHAT IS LEADERSHIP?

Cindy is a physician and a leader in health equity and family medicine. She has trained in Zen leadership for a number of years and teaches in the HEAL program. She also sits on the board of a philanthropic organization that funds various community health initiatives. At one such board meeting, she and others had just heard a presentation for a $1 million program to prevent childhood obesity. The presenters had put a lot of thought into it, and Cindy expressed that their proposal was well worth funding. A fellow board member, known for getting wound up at times and hard to stop, started speaking out against it, not because of its deficiencies, but because of outside factors having nothing to do with the proposal. The Board Chair wasn't sure what to make of the discord, but said if the members could not agree, the project would not go forward.

Normally, Cindy was a quiet voice on this board and, in the past, she might have let this board member bully her. But not on this day. Settling deeply into her center, she spoke up, saying the board was confusing separate matters, and needed to consider the project on its own merits. She made a motion to approve the project, and suggested they take a break and come back afterwards for a vote. She rightly sensed that people needed a breather, and she put the break to good use by engaging the difficult board member. She spoke with confidence and also heartfelt connection. "You raise good points," she told him, "yet they are outside the scope of this project. You and I have seen so many programs. As county-wide programs go, this is as good as it gets." When the board reconvened after the break, the troublesome board member himself seconded the motion to approve the project.

Cindy's simple act of leadership did not come from position power, but from resonating with the whole picture, including sensing its timing and the need for a breather, and acting for the sake of the whole. Several board members later came up to Cindy to express their gratitude for her intervention, and even the objecting board member felt heard and respected, further signs of Cindy's functioning from a state of wholeness that inspired rather than offended.

There are many definitions of leadership, but the one I want to explore in this chapter is what Cindy modeled. Kevin Cashman aptly defined this quality of leadership as "authentic self-expression that creates value." The question is what "self" do we express and how authentically can we express it? Zen blasts through the grasping, frightened ego self, giving rise to what we define as Zen leadership: authentic expression of the whole Self that creates wondrous value.

Leadership of this quality raises people up. It is leadership that gives life to the people and situations around it. A couple years ago, Cindy accepted an even bigger job as head of a Department of Family Medicine at another major university. Within a month of her arrival, during her morning walk-through of the department's bullpen where she would greet each person, a seasoned employee spoke up, "You have no idea how much happier people are since you've arrived. You've lifted the spirits of this entire department. We're so glad you're here!" "I haven't done anything," Cindy protested in her warm way. "But you have," came the response. "You see us. You talk to us. You hear us." You can bet Cindy is resonating with this entire department and getting them resonating as one.

But perhaps this strikes you as a soft way to lead. Maybe it doesn't seem as powerful as leaders who use their position to make people snap into line, or keep people "on their toes" through fear and intimidation. Maybe it doesn't seem as galvanizing as leaders who grab attention through sensationalism, or drag people down to their most primitive, tribal origins by stoking their fears. Aren't those examples of leadership, too? I get asked this question in leadership programs, and write at a time when glaring examples of this kind of leader are tearing at our social fabric, polarizing our politics, and poisoning our dialogue. It sort of looks like leadership because it commands so much attention and certainly makes a difference. Yet it's coming from a primitive, egocentric stage of development. In this day and age, at least in developed countries, we have developed well beyond that stage, so it represents something of a throwback: the destruction of value. It's like kicking a ball downhill and claiming credit for it rolling: it's easy to bring people down, and hard to lift them up toward their greater selves. It's easy to stoke fear and hard to take fear away.

From a resonance perspective, it's clear that one can create an enormous amplification of signal by playing to people's fears and regressing them to a place they once grew up through. In fact, some leaders use this as a strategy and we see it all over social media. It's a good way to grab attention because negative emotions grab our attention even more strongly than do positive ones. But I would not call it leadership in the largest sense because it is ultimately egocentric, not universal. And even though such leaders can make a big splash at the time, history tends to judge fear-based leaders accordingly. There's a different place in history for leaders like Lincoln, Gandhi or Mandela who unite rather than divide. This is not a good-vs.-evil, or left-vs.-right argument; the way we eat energy as dissipative structures creates a natural evolutionary direction that embraces and includes expanding consciousness. Ken Wilber characterizes this progression as egocentric to group-centric to world-centric to Kosmos-centric (i.e., universal). Dan Siegel characterizes it as higher levels of integration inseparably connected to our well-being, starting with personal consciousness, and then spanning states, people, time, space, and all dimensions. We evolve toward *wholeness*. And the kind of leadership that adds value and makes a difference in the direction of this wholeness is what moves us forward in our personal and collective journey. That is the kind of leadership we need in abundance, and we explore that leadership here.

REALIZING GOALS AND DREAMS

Bob found an outstanding mentor when he was still a teenager: an Aikido teacher who wouldn't let him on the mat if he didn't also train in Zen. He admired this teacher, so he started training in both, loving Aikido and more or less putting up with Zen. When his teacher quite suddenly died, Bob carried on the dojo and, though just in his twenties, he grew it with skill and sincerity. Over the years, he also completed a doctorate in movement science and started teaching at a local college. By then, mind-body training and teaching was deep in his bones, and something started gnawing on him that wouldn't let go of: too many of the young people he saw every day were simply lost.

Some of the causes were obvious: "They aren't clear where they're going, even as they get deeply in debt, or their parents get in debt with a mountain of expectations they can't fulfill," Bob explains. Some of the causes are less obvious and more pervasive: young people today are growing into a world where, in most fields, technology is likely to supplant the majority of current jobs[52], where artificial intelligence is likely to surpass human intelligence before they're 50[53]. If they live in the United States, they're witnessing mass murders, including in schools, as a regular news event. All the while, the planet is heating up, while they watch the generations before them attempt to maintain the untenable status quo. No wonder there's a deep anxiety among young people!

A dream started taking shape in Bob to help young people find their way. In some ways he was already doing that as a college professor, but he was frustrated that he was tackling the problem on too small a scale. All of which he shared with his friend, Don, while on a hike up Wachusett Mountain one day. Don, with a mind for scale, suggested developing an online program. That lit Bob up, and thus was born the idea for *Ignite Your Way*, a coaching-assisted virtual way to help young people anywhere get a grip on their gifts and goals, and what they could do to realize them. Bob was a natural teacher for the project, and his enthusiasm further inspired Don to become its financial backer. When Bob told me about it, I, too, could hear the energy in his voice and feel the "rightness" of this project for this person at this time. That's the signature of resonance. And that's what we need to listen for, or feel, in sizing up goals and dreams and decide whether they're worth pursuing.

We can return to our basic definition of resonance in Chapter 1 as a good guide to furthering our goals and dreams. I've repeated it in Figure 7-1, adapted to our human-scale ideas. The white bubbles depict what we may be saying or thinking; the grey bubbles are examples of what we may be hearing or sensing. In a way, we're asking, when we "strike" this idea, is "Does it ring? Do *we* ring? Do others ring with us?" Recall, from the example of shouting into the strings of a grand piano, that while we can't predict what will resonate in complex systems, resonance reveals itself in the build-up of energy when vibrations match. When an idea matches us, our vibratory signal is one of greater coherence that can be heard in our voice, seen in our body language, and felt as enthusiasm. When it further matches a need that others sense, too, they will sense our energy for it, and the idea itself will strike a resonant chord in them.

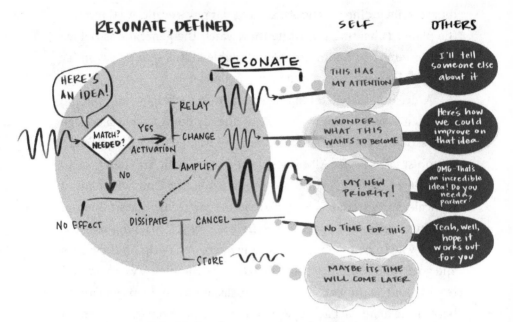

Figure 7-1. How ideas resonate in ourselves and others

Catching resonance is the first step in realizing what an idea can become, and applies to every step in the process of "concretizing" that idea. You can think of realizing your goals and dreams—or leadership in general—as turning the energy of ideas into concrete things that matter. From the world of lean startups and exponential organizations,[54] we can derive a simple model for moving from ideas into action—and ultimately outcomes—that makes these points for resonance clear, shown in Figure 7-2.

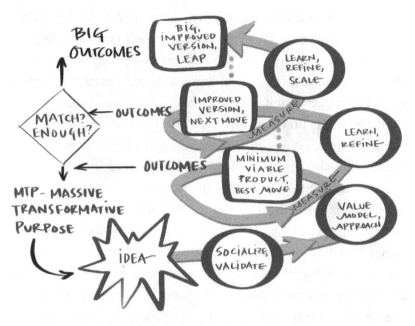

Figure 7-2. From ideas to outcomes: build, measure and learn

We start, as Bob did with sensitivity to conditions—kids are lost—that resonates into a purposefulness we need to act on: help young people find their way. In exponential organizations, this is called a Massive Transformative Purpose or MTP, and if it's truly massive, others will resonate with it as well. An idea forms around how to serve this purpose. In Bob's case it was an online course, and he started socializing this idea with friends and colleagues. Sparking even more resonance at that stage, he continued to refine it into a value model, that is, a concrete business model or approach for how he'd generate value for everyone connected to this venture, including customers, implementers and investors. Resonating at this stage meant that Bob attracted the partners and capital he needed to build a minimum viable product (MVP). Piloting his MVP with a small group generated some outcomes that Bob measured and paid close attention to—again, an example of resonance. He learned, for example, that a number of young people weren't finishing the program, and that he had to add some gaming-style features to better hook their motivation. Incorporating these learnings, he's now launching the next version of *Ignite Your Way* in a spiral of build-measure-learn that is the hallmark of successful startups. At some point, the product is mature enough that it's ready to scale, which often requires more capital for bigger production or widespread marketing and sales. The outcomes at each stage can be compared against the original massive purpose for whether it has been adequately served.

This same model can apply to non-profit efforts, services, or even dreams like being an astronaut. If I play my astronaut dream through this model, I can see exactly where resonance stopped and things broke down. I had this idea to be an astronaut—probably driven more by a personal need for adventure and self-worth than by any truly massive transformative purpose. But like many others, I did see space at the frontier of human possibility: a uniting force. And my idea was validated by living in a country and at a time when space travel became a new frontier, eventually even for women.

My approach was to get NASA to give me my dream, and I made some good moves in that direction: I signaled my interest, applied to the program, accepted a job at NASA's Johnson Space Center, worked hard, learned how to fly, kept applying to the program. But what I didn't do was listen to outcomes, including in my own body. Moreover, I wasn't resonating a strong, clear signal because I was internally divided by feeling that I could never show my flaws, such as my breathtaking allergy to cats. Even in the crucial moments of the astronaut candidate interviews, many of my answers weren't ringing true because they weren't really *my* answers, but rather my best guess at which answer might get me the job. "If you were an animal, what kind of animal would you be?" I recall as one of the questions in my first interview. Am I giving it my authentic, from-the-heart answer? No, I'm not even in touch with what my from-the-heart answer would be, as my mind is whirling frantically to guess the correct answer: *hmm, let's see, this is a flight job so it should probably be a flying animal. . . . there's sort of a militaristic feeling around here so I'll say, "Eagle."* Bullshit. No one resonated with that.

You might think of a goal or dream that's important to you now and run it through this model and see where you are with it. Is it fueled by a massive purpose felt by others? Do you get energized talking about it and are others energized with you? Do you have a viable approach to it that you are all-in on? The answer doesn't have to be "yes," because listening to "no" is just as important. Not all ideas have to be acted upon. Indeed, ideas are a dime a dozen, and a more reliable test is to ask, "What idea is so compelling it won't let you go?" Listening, as you now know, is a crucial act of resonating with outer conditions and inner truths, and letting them change us. When we listen with curiosity or openness, new vibrations can change us internally, thus altering our priorities, actions, communication and connection with others. Likewise, acting all-in and all-out on our most compelling ideas—not half-assed or internally divided—is how our actions resonate at full strength.

We realize our goals and dreams by making them real through the spiral of trying something out, then listening for resonance in the outcomes, learning and adjusting our approach as we go—i.e., build (or do something), then measure, then learn. If we ever quit listening, it's like unplugging ourselves from external energy sources and running purely on battery power. It may carry us for a while, but eventually we'll wear down, and our moves will be increasingly out of sync with the conditions we're no longer paying attention to.

Even when we do keep listening, the further challenge is to discern whether what we're hearing calls for course correction or for perseverance. We may have to be patient through long stretches of little or no progress as we prime the pump, and muddle through early stages of latent change, where energy is getting stored in the system but it looks like nothing is happening. How can we tell the difference between necessary perseverance and tone-deaf stubbornness? We go back to the playground of our youth for an answer.

DRIVING RHYTHM

Can you picture a swingset you used to play on? I invite you to go there now in your imagination and feel what you'd do to get the swing going. You know that a bunch of flailing about and shaking your legs is just going to rattle the chains. It may feel like you're doing something, but it's not sensitive to the conditions. Rather, if your feet can touch the ground and walk a couple steps backward and simply let go, the swing will do its swing-thing. You also know that if you do nothing further, the energy of that initial oscillation will eventually dissipate and you'll be back at the bottom. But, if you keep sensing the rhythm of the system and pump your legs at the right time, you can add energy to each oscillation and keep going and going and going. Moreover, the felt sense of this process is harmonious and we register it as joy. No kid goes to the playground saying they have to put in a hard day's labor on the swingset. No, this is fun!

We can apply the same principles and look for the same felt sense in how we lead, create value, and realize our ideas. We can apply an effort, listen for the effect, and time or adjust our next move accordingly. Now a swing, by design, is a quickly responsive system and operates at a frequency easily within our attention span. It doesn't take a great deal of perseverance to get it going or patience to have fun on it—if it did, it would never have become a playground staple. But real-life conditions we lead in—from launching startups, to motivating teams, to inspiring change in large, lumbering systems, to healing divided communities—all have differing response rates and frequencies at which they *can* change. How can we adjust our leadership, as well as our expectations, to match conditions, and even have fun in the process? The *Driving Rhythm* practices (see box) are a good guide.

DRIVING RHYTHM

These practices aren't meant to be sequential or done once-and-for-all, but rather are points to keep checking yourself on, though I strongly suggest: start with the first one and go from there.

Become the system. Be one-with whatever system you're trying to create value within or for. Relax and feel yourself extend into this whole picture, and feel how this system would move as a part of your own body. If it were put to music, what would be its beat? What are some of the natural rhythms it operates with? Examples might be daily tag-ups, weekly updates, monthly reviews, or annual conferences. Where are its stuck points? Where is energy flowing?

Test responsiveness. Throw in a meaningful action—the equivalent of starting the swing or pumping your legs—and see what happens. Let go, get quiet and listen. Try a different action. Let go, get quiet and listen. Get a feel for where you're needing to get something new going, which may take some pump priming, versus where you can add to momentum already in the system and just pump the swing higher.

Feel for a responsive part. Even if the overall system is sluggish, look for some part of it where you can build resonance. It could be collaborating with a highly productive person, teaming up with a small group of change agents, or finding an early-adopting audience for your service. You're looking for something with the responsiveness of a swingset within the larger system, where your efforts have a visible effect. Or, better yet, something like a rudder on a ship where small movement can have a big effect.

(cont.)

Feel for what happens when nothing is happening. If you're in the phase of priming the pump in a sluggish system, you may go for some time where little is happening or obstacles outweigh progress. Relax, get quiet, and listen. Is your own energy and commitment steady or dissipating? Moments of discouragement are natural, but do you bounce back just as committed, or can you feel yourself like a swing slowing down? Is there still a natural need for this idea? Is there still an essential joy in pursuing it? If so, feel into that joy and, becoming the whole picture, ask what is your best advice to yourself?

Be wholly committed when acting. Whatever you do, do it wholeheartedly. That doesn't mean go to unnatural extremes or get caught up in perfectionism or adding bells and whistles. It means when you pump, pump with your whole being. Be-as-one—head, heart and *hara*—in all that you do. Your actions will be more clear, strong and coherent: you resonating at full strength.

Be wholly unattached to outcomes. This is tough, because you wouldn't put wholehearted effort into an idea or cause you didn't care deeply about. And yet, being unattached to outcomes is what enables you to see clearly, discern deeply, and adjust accordingly. Being unattached doesn't mean going aloof or spiritually bypassing. Rather, when discouragement or other negative emotions arise, move right into them, as in the *Taming Fear* practice (Chapter 5). Let them drop through your body, metabolizing them fully to the point of acceptance. Acceptance is the crucial pivot point that frees you from coping mode and enables you to continue adding value. Hold any expectations lightly, and be curious what's around the next bend. Starting from acceptance, it's a short trip to joy.

These practices help us find ways to bootstrap progress and maintain our resilience, even in the absence of progress. We bootstrap progress by finding the equivalent of a responsive swingset within a sluggish system where we can build some momentum. In change efforts or product launches, this is akin to creating an early win or finding early adopters. This is what Bob is working toward, for example, in finding an early-adopting school for *Ignite Your Way* that could become a case study for its success. From a resonance point of view, finding an initial swing you can pump provides crucial amplification of your idea so it can be heard by the next tier of people who are less sensitive or receptive.

A metaphor for this step is the art that is now emerging where people put super-sensitive microphones and amplifiers into farms and gardens to hear the sound of corn growing[55], or into great ceramic pots and vessels from antiquity to hear their intrinsic vibrational frequency[56]. Ordinarily, we humans can't hear these things, but with skillful amplification, everyone can hear them. Nascent ideas are the same way: they need skillful amplification.

As for maintaining resilience in the face of no progress, the core practice is to keep returning to your Self as the whole picture, not as a nice-to-think thought, but in the salient experience of Samadhi. Being unattached to the outcomes is also important, devilishly difficult as it is to do, because attachment pulls us into a smaller self stuck to a problem, locked in a battle. The equanimity and Witness perspective developed in Zazen really do help in being unflinchingly present for discomfort and breathing it down. As negative emotions arise— anger, frustration, discouragement—we do well to breathe right into them and feel them drop in our own body, as in the *Taming Fear* practice. Indeed, getting to the root of fear that underlies our negative emotions is what lets them sink into familiarity, raw sensation, and eventually, acceptance. Unattachment is not an air of "I don't care" but of total honesty with the facts at hand and supreme acceptance that it is what it is—and we are boundlessly bigger than it.

That said, everything changes in accordance with its nature and the forces holding it in place—regardless of our agenda. In that state of acceptance, we can enter the great dance with joy, matching rhythm, letting it change us, adding our drive on the beat and discovering, in partnership with life itself, which of our ideas are ready to happen.

RIGHT ENERGY, RIGHT TIME

Supporting us in this great dance is our inner team of energy patterns, which, between them, can match any beat. When it comes to creating value or turning the energy of ideas into things that matter, the energy patterns are indispensable, because they span the spectrum from antenna-dish sensing to laser-like acting, from largely resonating with others to being the force that causes others to resonate. As we described earlier, the energy patterns also represent deepening penetration of the manifesting flow of energy, physically resonating deeper in our bodies until we're all-in: thoughts, emotions and actions coherently aligned. Climbing the spiral of Figure 7-2, let's explore what each pattern has to offer. The order below is not the only order in which the patterns can be engaged, nor are they engaged once and for all. Indeed, like coloring with a box of crayons, we'll find ourselves going back and forth in what we select for each situation. But the order that follows gives a feel for the value created by the body-and-mindset of each, that we may become more agile and clear in using the right energy at the right time.

Visionary. The antenna dish of the patterns, Visionary's wide-ranging sensitivity, fuels imagination, ideation and creativity. It's the place we would start in sensing purpose, unmet needs, or future trends. It's also a pattern we would want to come back to as we pursue an idea and run into resistance. It has an intuitive sense for energy flow and can often help us find those responsive swing-like parts or people in otherwise resistive systems. Visionary also refuels our resilience with its bigness, its ability to let go and expand into Samadhi. As the most ethereal of the patterns, Visionary is where we want to return when matters are stuck and the energy of creativity is needed. But to get anything done, we need to descend from Visionary and engage the other patterns.

Collaborator. The rhythmic social animal of the patterns, Collaborator is a natural energy to bring in as we socialize our idea and see if enthusiasm builds. It is also the pattern with the best sense for rhythm, especially with people. We'll want to use it to sense timing, meeting people where they are, indeed, becoming one-with them in a handshake of mutual benefit. It is a pattern brimming with positive emotions, and can be a source of joy and comic relief amidst disappointment. Like water, it has a way of finding a way, and is a good energy to play with when we feel blocked or thwarted. But also like water, it is better at flow than finding the finish line.

Organizer. The disciplined engineer among the patterns, Organizer will take the big idea and people involved and build a process for creating value. Plans, checklists, business model templates, management of resources, and to-do lists of next steps are among its specialties. With its logical sense of how one thing leads to another, it may be the first pattern to pick out the metaphorical rudder on the ship where efforts can have an outsized effect. It will also be the first pattern to detect untidy loose ends of how an idea is becoming concrete and find process solutions to correct matters. Indispensable as it is, this is also the pattern that struggles the most to be unattached to outcomes or adjust plans when conditions have changed.

Driver. The fierce warrior of the team, Driver will push the idea across milestones of progress. Sometimes a disruptive flame-thrower, sometimes a great protector, it will not let the right idea die from complacency or bullshit. It's a pattern we'll want to engage to cut out distractions, eliminate flimsy barriers, and stand up for our idea when it counts. It will also unflinchingly examine outcomes to adjust its tactics for winning, holding us and others accountable (admittedly with some tendency to blame, which we need to be careful of). Grounded at the base of the *hara*, the Driver connects us fully with our power, and puts conviction into our movements. Only when ideas reach this base in us, do we radiate our most powerful signal, which can more readily bring about resonance in the outer world. That said, Driver needs Visionary to be ever on the lookout, so that it doesn't win the wrong battle.

Table 7-1 summarizes the indispensable role of each pattern in maturing an idea from pure energy into something that matters in our shared world. The fact that all patterns are needed while you and I have favorites, underscores the need for some intentionality in moving into patterns that are not our favorites. Which pattern could help you with an idea you're trying to realize now?

Table 7.1 Creating Value across the Four Energy Patterns

	DRIVER	ORGANIZER	COLLABORATOR	VISIONARY
Early Role	Protecting the idea, eliminating distractions, keeping pace, clarifying actions and targets	Shaping an approach, planning and/or processing around the idea, determining roles, resources, next steps	Building enthusiasm, sensing the right timing, socializing the idea and finding people who can help	Imagining, ideating, connecting to purpose, unmet needs, future trends, opening to possibility
Later Role	Disrupting status quo, holding accountability to outcomes, pushing to the finish	Taking disciplined measures, maintaining progress and quality, adjusting processes and plans	Maintaining enthusiasm and network of support, finding way around obstacles, feeling for rhythm and timing	Sensing changing conditions and larger forces to work with, letting go, opening into Samadhi bigness

LEAD THE WAY

This simple phrase—Lead the Way—has become something of a tagline for us at IZL, as it captures the quality of *wu-wei* (effortless effort) that is creating value and making a difference in accordance with the Way. We capitalize "Way" to emphasize it's not just any old way, but a way that is in harmonious resonance with universal energy. It's not just my idea, but an idea that resonated with me, and may well resonate with you. It's not me leading, it's large-scale inspiration informing my actions, just as it may inform yours. Leading becomes not me telling you what to do, but connecting us both to something larger. Just as a sensitive poet may be the first to find words for something emerging in the Zeitgeist, a leader of the Way may be the first antenna to pick up a signal of something ready to happen and show it to others.

The challenge in leading this way is that the Way does not stop, and our mind often does. We get attached to our creature comforts, the people we love, our way of life, job security, financial stability—all those conditions we've cobbled together to get our needs met. Being responsive to the Way doesn't mean all those things go out the window, but it can mean change in any of them. Resistance to this change is natural, as Joseph Campbell beautifully articulates as the Hero's Journey, exemplified in stories from Homer's *Odyssey* to *Star Wars*. While step one in the Journey is "hearing the call", it is quickly followed by step two: "rejecting the call.[57]" Why do we reject it? Because even though we've heard it and started vibrating with it, it doesn't match life as we know it, so it encounters internal resistance.

In a micro sense, I encountered this resistance even as the idea for this book hit me. I know how much time it takes me to write a book, I know how many other people and things get put on the back burner, and here I'm running IZL and teaching all over the world. How do I possibly make time for this? What my training has taught me is to simply "sit with" questions like this, which is not to say "think about them" during sitting, but instead let the question percolate subconsciously as I sit morning after morning, and see what happens. My commitment is: if this idea is right for me, I will let it change me. I will let it reorganize my priorities, my day and the people in it, whatever it takes, and trust that nothing else truly right for me will be irrecoverably compromised. As I wrote about in *The Zen Leader*, this is exactly how we bring an idea or vision from the future into the present: we change our self[58]. And because we exist in the present, as soon as we exactly match the self of that idea, that idea is manifest in the present. It can't be anywhere else. Conversely, if we can't match that self, the idea will not manifest.

This willingness to be open, curious, and let life change us is not just the hallmark of Zen leadership, but of any leader of innovation, which pretty much means any successful leader today. I teach leadership programs for a corporate client that has launched a company-wide campaign to develop more innovative leaders. In these leadership programs, participants learn about themselves and receive written feedback from colleagues on their strengths and weaknesses. I'm struck by how often the trait of openness in a leader further inspires others who say they this leader makes them feel heard and able to explore new ideas. Conversely, in leaders who are not open, I read things like, "stuck in the past," "doesn't listen," or "seems to have mind already made up." Rather than build resonance, leaders who aren't open to being changed dissipate energy, and their teams become less engaged.

We may know the importance of openness intellectually, but still face resistance in changing ourselves, and even more in the cumbersome, corporate systems we're a part of. Companies attribute the resistance to new ideas as a fear of failure, but I would say it's deeper than that: a stubborn ego doesn't want to relinquish any of the mooring lines it knows itself by. To give up any one of them feels like a little death. This is true even for an individual ego, and gets even more reinforced by the collective ego of an organization as represented in its culture. The irony, of course, is that to *not* cut some of those mooring lines to the past leads to certain obsolescence. That's why it becomes so critical to know our selves beyond the ego. That's why leaders in organizations must be able to envision the future beyond the current culture. When we know we're the whole picture, we can hold any part of it lightly, and keep adapting to what's present.

To lead the Way is to commit to listening to life, to match the energy of conditions. To use a sailing analogy, it is to commit to listening to the wind and adjusting ourselves, our course and sails accordingly. It's not the only way to sail, but it is the only way to sail well. The irony in leading the Way is that it is the easiest and hardest way to lead. It is easiest in that it's always appropriate, not clumsy, and it is simply joyful to do the right thing at the right time. It makes exactly the difference that is ready to be made, extinguishing fear, and being inexhaustibly resilient. It is also hard, in that it calls for the greatest sensitivity to conditions and agility in our mind-body system, and that only comes through repeated practice. Yet, a challenge I make to myself and would make to you as well is: what the heck else do we have to do? It's become painfully clear to me that if I'm doing anything wrapped up in my own stuff and not matching conditions around me, I'm spinning my wheels. Plus, as we've seen, practice can be both deep and intensive as well as available in any moment. Drop into our center, lengthen our exhale, relax our eyes to 180-degrees and listen for what stirs in this moment. Leading the Way is not far away.

Good thing, because it also the Way of inspiring the greatest resonance in those around us, which is our next stop.

RESONANCE RECAP—LEADERSHIP

- Leadership is authentic self-expression that creates value; Zen leadership, is authentic expression of the whole Self that creates wondrous value.
- The energy of ideas turns into things that matter through resonance, in a spiral of build (or try something), measure, learn.
- Driving rhythm and matching conditions are key to how we make a difference with resilience and joy.
- We embody the necessary agility for driving rhythm by applying the right energy pattern at the right time.
- To lead (according to) the Way is both easy and hard, yet is the only way to lead well.

8

TEAMS

S omething special happens in a group after about two days of the intensive Zen training that is *sesshin*. It comes together in a kind of flow state—a group Samadhi—where an unspoken harmony arises in the way people converge on a doorway, lay out their shoes, or sort out the morning chores. United in the purpose to create optimal training conditions for all, the group generally becomes not only a team, but a high-performing one, where the strength of human bonds defy logic.

That *sesshin* induces flow is no surprise. We know from studies of the flow state in individuals and in the workplace, which we review in this chapter, that it's triggered through a combination of intense challenge and support, both of which are present in *sesshin*. But what flow represents in teams is a phase shift, where resonance not only amplifies the efforts of individuals, but quite suddenly shifts into an entirely new condition, not unlike when ice melts into water or metal becomes superconducting. So, while an individual may be capable of pumping a swing, it's the resonance among people that opens up vast new horizons. If your goals are, as Jim Collins advises, "big, hairy and audacious"[59] or your dreams are large, they will call for such collective effort. From resonance in choirs that brings out harmonics that no individual voice is making, to teams that outperform the capabilities of any individual on them, we'll look at examples of how the whole becomes greater than the sum of its parts. You'll learn what's needed for individual efforts to add up in teams, and to prime the pump for the phase-shifting "magic" of resonance to emerge.

THE SEAL MERGE

Steven Kotler and Jamie Wheal open *Stealing Fire* with an engaging tale of resonance: how a Navy SEAL team pulled off the successful capture of Al-Qaeda operative in Afghanistan[60]. What stands out in this story is not the heroism or military strategy. Yes, these were incredibly well-trained men with a clear mission: to capture their "target" alive. They had well-conceived plans and contingencies to those plans, all committed to memory, all ready to go. And when they received word that the target had stopped for the night, go they did.

All that might be expected. But still, a "special sauce" was missing that would be essential for their success, "the only way to get the job done," in the words of the Rich Davis, the not-real name of the SEAL team commander. They had only a mile to hike to reach their target, and he hoped it would be enough for them to *merge*, that is, to make what he called "the switch" where they stopped being individuals and became connected-as-one. An individual might blow the mission with a twitchy trigger finger. But in this hive mentality, intelligence was multiplied and fear had no room to grow. "More than any other skill," Davis explained, "SEALs rely on this merger of consciousness. Being able to flip that switch—that's the real secret to being a SEAL." He would also acknowledge that it's not well understood or something everyone can do. Part of SEAL screening puts people into high stakes, back-against-the-wall conditions to see if they merge with others or retreat into themselves. According to Kotler and Wheal, nearly 80% of SEAL candidates are screened out.

But this SEAL team was made of mergers. And on that night, as they moved out toward their target, Davis could see and feel that the team did make the switch: "the invisible mechanism locking, the group synchronizing as we patrolled. . . . To look at it from a distance it would seem choreographed." They went on to make a flawless capture with not a bullet fired. If we could have jumped in with EEG caps, we could have, no doubt, seen them all on the same wavelength. We could have seen that each had made internal maps of the others, of the team as a whole, so that when one patrol looked left, the other looked right, without the delay of thought, much less second guessing. We may well have measured an electromagnetic field shift when they made the switch into their group Samadhi, and we may have conjectured that being in the presence of that altered field contributed to their subjective experience of an altered state, what the Greeks called *ecstatis* or "stepping beyond oneself."

While such measures were not made that night in Afghanistan, they are increasingly being made to better understand or even "hack into" altered states of consciousness[61]. Indeed, "stepping beyond oneself" into flow or Samadhi feels so good, it is the very fire that *Stealing Fire* tries to give us easier access to. The irony is that the "I" who wants altered states or flow, or better yet, a shortcut to them, is the crystalized ego that resists vibrating with universal energy available to it, even now. To become one-with, a sort of melting or merge has to occur in which "I" temporarily forgets itself or is a willing participant. Mihaly Csikszentmihalyi called this "flow" to capture this sense of moving with, in contrast to the crystalline solidity of a stand-apart "I"[62]. Otto Scharmer likens it to "breaking through a membrane," where "I don't matter so much as an individual anymore. Yet, paradoxically, I'm more of an individual at the same time."[63] What makes us forget ourselves or be willing to melt?

THE CONNECTED WISDOM OF TEAMS

Teams are often the first place we experience it—that dropping into flow or a group Samadhi (terms I'll use interchangeably to mean a vibrationally coherent group state). Teams by their nature involve factors conducive to entering flow as they come together around a common purpose or unifying challenge, which calls for individual concentration as well as interdependent support[64]. Whether we're on a sports team trying to win a championship, a work team launching a radical new service, or a choir in a pivotal performance, when the target demands our full concentration and we need and feel supported by the rest of the team, we are more likely to forget ourselves and merge into something larger. Of course, we also have to be capable of acting in accord with the team's purpose, which calls for individual agency, prior training, and ongoing feedback and learning. Additionally, for the team to act as one, it has to have ways to get individual efforts to add up to group coherence. On a sports team, this might be a set of team plays practiced so often as to become reflexive. On a work team, these might be team processes around how work is shared and progress is measured. In a choir, we could say it's literally getting on the same page of music.

From a resonance perspective, teams can set up a virtuous cycle between individual coherence and group coherence, where each affects the other and the strongest, most coherent signal can entrain the others. Just as parts of the brain can add up to strong brainwave coherence, and just as the brainwaves between people can add up in coherent communication, so the human-waves of a team can add up to a signal strong enough to sync up the stragglers. Again, this collective coherence is not mysterious or just a human phenomenon: a bunch of pendulum clocks oscillating in the same room would sync up the same way. What *does* make it special, however, is the wondrous complexity of what human teams can accomplish, plus the wondrous subjective experience of being on such a team.

The experience is one of expanded consciousness, connection to a wisdom beyond oneself and the sheer joy of accessing it. It often pulls out of people capabilities or determination they didn't know they had. Indeed, in the classic, *The Wisdom of Teams*, one of the features distinguishing a high-performing team—what we would call a team in flow—from an ordinary team was that it radically outperformed expectations given who was on it[65]. And what was the "special sauce" that made a team able to shift into this mode? Not unlike the SEAL team, it was an emotional cohesion that would not leave anyone behind or let anyone fail. The research into flow on teams finds the same thing. As flow researcher Gyongyi Kallai puts it, "The high cohesion of a team in flow is like a nest you don't let anyone fall out of." One can imagine how emotional unity on a team could also magnify its impact, much as wholeheartedness strengthens the electromagnetic field of an individual. In the experience of connectedness, fear falls away and love expands. No wonder we're able to do together what we would never be able to do alone.

What's more, we're able to create together what we cannot create alone, namely the countless possibilities that emerge through the harmonies of multiple voices or players. From complex, multi-player maneuvers in sports, to dividing and conquering a team challenge, to the soaring harmonies of a choir singing, the relationship *between* systems vibrating together becomes its own creation. And because it emerges from a more expansive state of consciousness than the individual ego, it represents an evolution of order that is exactly the growth direction of our healthy, well-functioning selves. So, when Dan Siegel puts ten singers on a stage and gives them a way for their voice-signals to add up—namely, a common piece of music—they self-organize into a spine-tingling rendition of "Amazing Grace." They could have all sung the same notes, but they don't, because when one has the skill to sing complex harmonies, it's more fun and interesting to rise to the challenge.

The same self-organizing principles apply to teams generally, and the conditions in which individuals dissolve their separate membranes and merge into something greater. Combining the research around flow and teamwork with what we know about resonance, we can distill four essential principles behind team flow:

Unifying challenge. There has to be a "why" for coming together, and a challenge formidable enough to demand full concentration. This would be the necessity that fuels invention, or the "burning platform" that makes an incontrovertible case for change. In the research around high-performing teams, Katzenberg and Smith found that adversity ("We're screwed!") was often the trigger for kicking the team into a higher gear. Necessity and adversity come together in what makes SEAL teams merge. From a resonance perspective, full concentration gives rise to brainwave coherence, which strengthens the individual's contribution to group coherence. It also gives rise to an intense listening for signals or data related to the task at hand, which stretches our antenna into more subtle ranges of sensing, expanding us out into something greater. Back-against-the-wall, we go big, not small.

Interdependence. Complementary skills have long been identified as a key component of what makes teams work, enabling teammates to play off one another, create harmonies together, and mitigate weaknesses. But this is just the starting point for building the trust and love that underlie interdependence. No one left behind, others having your back, you having their backs, being essential to the rest of the team, no one let down and no one to let down: these qualities of interdependence move us "beyond oneself" into a something greater where we can evolve our order. The team serves as something of a local necessity for conducting universal energy through our more-connected Self. Physically, as we become one-with each person on the team and the team as a whole, we're making interior maps of them, literally embodying a representation of them, which becomes an enlarged landscape out of which thought arises and mind makes choices around how to direct energy. In terms of resonance, interdependence gives rise to synchronized communication ("getting on the same wavelength") and creative harmonies.

Personal Agency. While group dynamics are crucial to group flow, each member must also have the agency to act. In organizational terms, this can be thought of as autonomy and empowerment—being authorized to think and act on their own[66]. This does not mean everyone can do their own thing, but rather, each person can resonate with their context and act spontaneously without going up and down a chain of command. This keeps energy flowing without crystallizing a separate "I" that gets stuck in doubt or fear or countermanded by others. The capability to act also implies sufficient skills and training to do the actions called for, as well as an ongoing ability to get feedback, learn and adjust. From seeing how resonance works in the body, we know that training builds pathways that can operate reflexively, while learning opens one to resonate with changing conditions. Both are needed for personal agency.

A Way to Add Up. The final piece to team flow is a way for individual efforts to add up so the whole team becomes "superconducting." A potent source of this integrating force is leadership within the team, which in this context would be someone generating a strong field, someone who goes into flow early and radiates a clear, coherent signal around which others resonate. Kallai calls these "flow agents" and has measured the five personality traits most associated with flow agents in the workplace: self-transcendence, cooperativeness, self-directedness (which includes openness), risk tolerance and persistence[67]. Structural elements are also important to getting efforts to add up, starting with clear, measurable goals and ways of getting ongoing feedback around progress. Team norms and processes also support adding up, from values and rules of engagement that "we all know," to metaphorical assembly lines that collect individual efforts into something greater.

A way to add up can be a conductor and common sheet music, in the case of an orchestra or choir. Here, too, leadership matters. Without a conductor, orchestras slow down and play to a least common denominator. In the presence of a great conductor, the same players spring music to life[68]. It was said of the great conductor, Wilhelm Furtwängler, that musicians played better the moment he walked into an auditorium. Likewise, strongly coherent leadership more quickly moves a team into flow and amplifies the effectiveness of team actions. This leadership can come from one strong flow agent, or it can be largely self-organized from the expanded consciousness of the Samadhi itself. SEAL teams on the move, for example, shift leadership to whoever knows what to do next.

These same principles—a unifying challenge, interdependence, personal agency and a way to get efforts to add up—are also at work in large scale social change, as we'll see the next chapter, but it's easy to see how they coalesce more readily in a small group than a large one, making it easier for a team to get in flow than for an entire organization or community. Little wonder that teams have become the unit of performance in most organizations. And little wonder that people who have worked on a team in flow often cite it as the most professionally satisfying work of their career.

BUILDING TEAM RESONANCE

Given the joy of "stepping beyond oneself" into a team in flow and the optimal performance that results, it's not surprising that people and organizations have wanted to figure out how to get more of this, which has spawned a good deal of research. We now know the sort of traits that characterize flow agents. Kallai has also characterized traits that make an organization more "fit for flow," which include autonomy and empowerment, opportunities for development, concentration, interdependence and, most of all, flow-agent type leaders[69]. Good to know, yet it would be a mistake to think we can clinically engineer flow-inducing conditions. That's not how it works. In a unifying challenge, necessity is either there or it isn't—it's not something we make up. We either do merge with others or we don't—it's not something that happens by edict. Just as we can't will ourselves into Samadhi, but only create conditions conducive for it arising, so it is with flow in teams.

We are hampered in understanding flow by the biases of our Western, objective, matter-based frame in which we're all in our separate skins with billiard-ball effects on one another. Flow is much easier to understand when we flip this around to an energy-based frame in which we're in constant vibration with our context, with choice and habits around how and with whom we resonate. So I'll use an energy-based frame to talk about how we might serve as flow agents and engender flow on a team. Being an agent implies our personal involvement in sensing the energies around us and generating a strong signal ourselves. So this is not a purely objective process, but rather a subjective *vibrating with* that opens up expanded, coherent consciousness through a team.

The energy patterns can be a useful guide for opening up or focusing the energy needed to help a group into flow. Just as shifting between patterns changes our individual energy from its broadest sensing to its most focused action, so the patterns can shift team energy. Sometimes in shifting energy, we'll find a better "frequency" for group coherence. And sometimes agility itself will help a group merge. Agility is like loosening the gears in a grandfather clock and allowing it a little more variability in how it oscillates so it can more readily synchronize with its fellow clocks in the room. So, here are some of the essentials each pattern contributes to getting or keeping a team in flow.

Visionary. This expansive, far-reaching, broadly sensing pattern is the "flow-iest" of the energy patterns and can be a gateway to group Samadhi. This is a pattern of self-transcendence and openness that most readily gives rise to connected wisdom and imagination. It's the leading energy in Otto Scharmer's Theory U exercise, a version of which is included in this chapter, for getting a group to "let go" into a connected state and "let come" collective inspiration. It is the pattern to sense patterns, to think far-out into the future and strategically across many moving parts or complex dynamics.

Collaborator. This positive, rhythmic, pattern engenders the most emotionally bonding energy on the team. Not surprisingly, many classic teambuilding activities are designed to bring out this quality of energy, from rocks and ropes courses where trust is built by not letting anyone fall, to bowling and drinking together. The spirit of leaving no one behind and always looking out for your teammates comes from this energy, as does the pick-ourselves-up resilience of recovering from setbacks.

Organizer. This is the energy that gets enough process in place for efforts to add up. It is the disciplined training and persistence that builds individual and team mastery. Organizer energy can parse a collective inspiration (or an immediate necessity) into next steps and concrete roles for each person to play. This conscientious, responsibility-taking pattern will measure progress, stabilize what's been gained or won, and bring quality and sincerity into the team's work.

Driver. This is the pattern that understands necessity and emergency, and can cut out distractions faster that you can say "PAY ATTENTION!" As the powerful *hara*-first integrator of our individual body, it supports our most all-in, all-out concentration on which flow depends. It can likewise do this in a team by keeping the unifying challenge front and center, and helping the team stay riveted on the most essential priorities in the moment.

Signs that a team could use more of a certain energy and ways to cultivate it are summarized in Table 8-1. Some of these cultivation practices are further described in *Inviting Team Resonance* (see box).

Just as EEG studies show us that brainwaves have to slow down in order to become coherent within an individual, so it is that practices that help a group cohere often start by slowing down, stepping back, or finding a way to get in rhythm. A SEAL team might do it by hiking together. A group of meditators might do it by breathing together, giving each breath an audible count from one to ten. A work team might take a pause when it's feeling stuck or on the cusp of an important decision and take a few deep *hara* breaths together.

You can experience this principle of slowing down to get in sync by having a group stand in a circle and hold hands. When I do this with IZL groups, I start by asking everyone to do their own thing—wave their hands or sway about however they want. The result, of course, is chaos. Then I ask everyone to stop, listen, and do nothing until they simply feel a rhythm coming through the group. Invariably, a slow wave of rhythm emerges and passes from person-to-person, sort of a group equivalent to a slow delta wave. I then ask everyone to stay in sync with that signal and add their own part. The result has a higher-level order that is simply more fun to do because each person can feel both connected and creative at the same time—a good thing to remember when you feel a team coming apart at the seams.

Table 8-1. Signs that a Team Needs More of a Pattern and Ways to Cultivate It

	DRIVER	ORGANIZER	COLLABORATOR	VISIONARY
Signs that a team needs more of this energy	Challenge or priorities unclear Too many distractions Moving too slowly Lack of accountability Outside forces threatening the team	Efforts not adding up Errors, sloppiness Unfinished tasks, missed milestones Insufficient feedback or listening Lack of discipline or persistence	Lack of bonding, trust, warmth Too rigid or stuck in problems Lack of fun, positive energy Needing to influence, engage others	Lack of inspiration or imagination Not seeing big picture, patterns Not open enough Risk-averse Too rigid or stuck

(cont.)

	DRIVER	ORGANIZER	COLLABORATOR	VISIONARY
Ways to cultivate on team: Meetings, communication	Fast meetings (e.g., stand-up, huddle) to sync up on priorities, next play Brief "bullet point" messaging, leading with key point	Put discipline into meetings (e.g., preparation, notes, follow up) Get data, increase feedback availability	Make emotional connection, get real Use stories, tell stories, find out user stories Argue opposite points of view to build empathy Circle up, pass a talking piece Celebrate!	Allow open time in meetings for brainstorming, reflection, wandering around Group visioning exercises, a la Theory U Share vision, meaning, patterns, big picture
Norms, Processes	Cut out BS and low priority work Cut processes in half	Slow down Listen Clean up "loose ends" in processes	Laugh it off, roll with the punches Make processes practical, pragmatic	Open up, let go of past Make processes light and adjustable to conditions
Physical environment	Remove distractions Make stark, use high contrast colors, red Music with driving beat (i.e., thrust on the beat)	Make status and progress visible Create spaces that are orderly and quiet Calm, classical music (i.e., held in step on the beat)	Create warm, fun places for people to gather Use bright colors, toys, things to pick up and play with Rhythmic music (i.e., to swing or sway to)	Bring the outside in, open imaginative spaces where people can wander, work alone or with others New Age music (i.e., expansive)
Physical activities to do together	Drop into *hara*, *hara* breathing Fast, challenging exercises or sports Drumming	Meditate Breathe as one, counting exhales aloud from 1 to 10 Walk matching steps	Teambuilding, trust-building activities with emotion, fun Singing, chanting Rhythmic drumming, dancing	180-degree vision Get out in nature Meditate Energy work; e.g., Tai Chi, Chi Gong, Yoga

INVITING TEAM RESONANCE

Here are a number of ways to build resonance in a group by establishing common rhythms or coherent communication.

- **Walking**—Walk in a single file line, with each person matching the rhythm of the person in the lead. Change who's in the lead and feel the difference in the walk.

- **Three hara breaths**—Take a pause in the team's activities by standing up and taking three, deep, slow *hara* breaths (as in Chapter 3, Figure 3-2), letting each exhale extend longer while still keeping the group together. This can be a valuable reset when the team is feeling stuck, or right before an important action.

- **Sitting Zazen**—Sit together for five to twenty minutes before diving into the team's agenda.

- **Breathing from one to ten**—Alternatively or in conjunction with *Zazen*, synchronize breathing by giving each exhale an audible count from one to ten. Encourage each person to send the sound of their audibly numbered exhale down to their *hara* and, from there, to let it radiate out to the group (as in Chapter 4, Figure 4-5).

- **Sharing Purposeful Stories**—This three-round exercise starts by working in pairs. Going one at a time, each person shares a personal story related to the team's purpose and their own role in it. For example, it could be a story about their own purpose for being on the team, or a story about a time when they made their best and fullest contribution. Partners can take notes if they like, as they'll be relaying this story in the next round. In the second round, pairs of partners group into foursomes, and partners share the story

(cont.)

they heard with the other two. In the final round, the team comes back into one big group and each person shares something of their experience in hearing the stories of others, as well as their own.

- **Circle up**—In this powerful, traditional practice, the group sits in a circle, and one or two questions for reflection and response are posed to the group. A talking piece is passed from person-to-person—we use a rock in IZL programs— and only the person with the talking piece may speak. This invites deeper listening on the part of the rest of the group. The talking piece can be passed serially around the group or, when the group is building on one another's wisdom, passed to the person who has something to say next, until each person has spoken once.

FLOW AGENTS IN AN ORGANIZATION

Kristi, the physician you met in Chapter 6, is not the only one from her healthcare system who has trained in IZL's HEAL programs. Three others have now come through—Gabe, Audrey and Katie— and I spoke with all of them recently to learn how they've applied the training in their organization, and what's been the effect of having now four of them resonating in a new way. Their answers were intriguing and instructive for how flow agents can work to change an organization.

"As soon as we got back from HEAL," Kristi opened, "I was in program implementation mode." As physicians who also train residents and supervise interns, these doctors have an influential role on the next generation of practitioners. According to Kallai's research, when flow agents are in influential positions, as these four are, flow spreads much more readily throughout the organization. But it didn't spread by pushing a new program. "We tried doing a three-hour session for residents," sharing some of the Zen practices for presence and connection with patients, "But it wasn't quite received," Kristi said. "So, since then I've dropped into more reading the situation, what's happening, what's needed, what are the unspoken requests. And then letting the training emerge in situations as they arise. This has been a real transition for me. It's like we're cross-pollinating a more centered, connected way of being in everything we do." Audrey added a musical analogy: "It's like we're harmonizing now, instead of sight-reading." It's a great example of how sensitivity opens up resonance in a way that just importing a learning may not.

Director of the residency program, Gabe, came back from HEAL and re-did her office. Out went the desk and in came four meditation cushions, along with a couple of chairs. Her office became the talk of the floor, as people tried to figure out what to make of it. "But it became such an invitation to sit down and have a real conversation," she said, that people grew fond of it. "Now lots of residents and clinical staff come to sit. Most of them still want to use the chairs, but the flow of conversation in the room is still different. Less formal, fewer barriers. More real." It's also become a ready place for colleagues to drop by and meditate, if only for a few minutes.

How has having several of them come through HEAL changed what they can do together? I asked. "It's easier to sing in a choir than a solo," Audrey responded extending her musical analogy. "We're so well connected, we can instinctively respond to one another," Kristi added, "I get a text from Gabe that says, 'Don't come to rounds today, I've got it' at exactly the moment when I needed some time freed up." Katie added, "I came back from HEAL feeling more energized and on purpose. Now I feel I can get in line with something bigger than myself that gets reinforced daily."

Their increased cohesion has also changed the environment around them. Others watch this foursome with a mix of bewilderment and "I'll have what she's having," as Kristi put it. Some feel that whatever goes on with those cushions in Gabe's office is just not for them, but there again, sensitivity helps as these four meet others where they are and model something others can resonate with. Kristi, for example, was attending rounds with new interns and could see how little they had learned about presence as opposed to having the "right answer." She snapped a photo of one of the interns to make her point. It showed the intern kneeling next to the patient's bed to have a heartfelt conversation, but kneeling right on the patient's oxygen hose, cutting it off. That day, the intern learned something more about what real presence means.

Even though they said they're not "pushing programs," what's clear is that the programs they're already teaching are resonating in a new way. "Residents tell me my teaching has changed," Katie said. "It happens more naturally and flows better. I feel a peace in the moment with no need to push—simply feeling the current." Meanwhile Kristi has seen enrollment in her Zen-based mindfulness elective become the norm. When she first offered it two years ago, no one signed up. Now, nearly all residents volunteer for it.

And what has been the effect on the larger organization? "We're a lot kinder than we used to be," Gabe answered. Years earlier, she had come through the very residency program she now directs, and says of the current program, "You wouldn't recognize it compared with what I came through. We have progressed so much. I think we would have gotten here eventually even if we hadn't done the training, but it probably would have taken us ten to fifteen years longer. . . . We're taking better care of patients, and better care of ourselves." Anonymous patent satisfaction scores would attest to the same thing. The percentage of patients who would "definitely" recommend this hospital has climbed to nearly 92%, more than ten points higher than before this team brought Zen leadership to bear. Written patient comments have also been uniformly positive over the past year, which is rare for any healthcare system, and something this foursome has a right to take joy in.

SENSING THE EMERGING FUTURE

We have no shortage of ideas among the creative people who lead our Wisconsin Chosei Zen dojo. And we take one another's ideas seriously, so when someone suggests starting a new program or buying a new building, it gets a fair hearing. Still, many ideas don't catch on: we talk about them for awhile, explore a few of their details, but the energy for them dies out. As it should. Not all ideas are meant to be implemented. As we saw in Chapter 7, a good measure of whether an idea is ripe to happen is whether it resonates with others as we socialize it. And within a team this is an even more reliable a measure.

So when the idea to buy an abandoned, 100-year old church in Madison came up, my first reaction was, *Here we go again.* Since I don't live in Madison, I wasn't as close to the question as others who train and teach there all the time. And the idea to buy a building had been floating around our board of directors for a number of years, with nothing quite catching on. Until this building. "It was as if the idea came fully formed," as Gordon Greene Roshi put it and, despite obstacles, enthusiasm kept growing. The zoning, for example, had to be changed, something that is never easy or assured, as anyone who has bought commercial property knows. But dojo members reached out to the community, inviting them in, showing how they could get involved in meditation or other classes, explaining how the building would be used and the need for a zoning change. The community was so pleased with the new life being breathed into this old building, they wrote a letter to the City Council in resounding support of the zoning change which passed unanimously. To this day, there is a rightness and fit between the dojo and the community that is increasingly populating morning meditation and other classes. This was a future ready to emerge, signaled by early resonance, first within the team, and expanding from there.

While we didn't follow any formalized process, one of the advantages of our dojo team is that we do meditate a great deal together and it's easy for us to sense energy and get on the same wavelength with one another. Otto Scharmer's Theory U is a more generalizable process for sensing a future ready to emerge, and is an excellent example of how resonance can build both within a team and with something greater[70]. The "U" of the Theory is a shift in consciousness that takes us out of everyday analytical mind to a more connected state that Scharmer calls "presencing"—short for sensing and bringing into the present (see Figure 8-1).

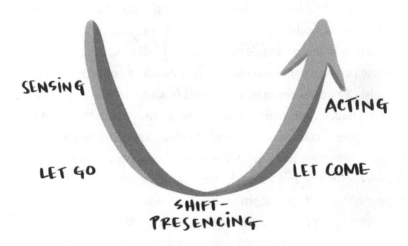

Figure 8-1. Theory U Model for Transformative Change

The U-turn of Theory U is a journey to and back from a more expanded consciousness from which the emerging future can be sensed. It calls for one to "let go" of ordinary ways of thinking and "let come" images, insights, ideas, no matter how surprising or disconnected they may seem. The process then completes by distilling themes into concrete actions. Source: O. Scharmer, Presencing Institute

The shift toward this more expansive consciousness starts with sensing in the expansive Visionary pattern, that is also able to "let go" of seeing things only as they've been. In Scharmer's terms, one "crosses a threshold" into a Samadhi state beyond what one can simply will—not unlike the merge of SEAL teams. In this open

Samadhi, we vibrate with an aspect of universal energy we might not ordinarily tune into that represents something ready to happen, the emerging future. But this future is not happening in the abstract to someone else. By virtue of the fact that we're vibrating with it, it represents a future that can emerge *through us*. From this expanded consciousness, we can then "let come" collective wisdom from that state, crystallizing it into action[71].

We'll look at an individual application of Theory U in Chapter 10 that is powerful in its own right. But when a group coheres around this process and builds collective wisdom around a jointly sensed signal it is, as Audrey put it, "easier to sing in a choir than solo," as well as rich in interdependent creativity. It is also a natural check and balance on what any individual may sense. In a collective Theory U exercise, a natural resonance emerges from multiple people sensing similar things. Again, not all ideas have to move to action, and what may be presenced could be signals to slow down and be patient. But whatever emerges has a chance to come from a more expansive level of consciousness and through multiple interpreting bodies. A way to apply Theory U in a team reflection, a practice that we've used to great effect at IZL, is given in the box (*Team Reflection Practice Based on Theory U*)[72]. More ways to apply it are available from Scharmer's Presencing Institute[73].

As useful as these practices are, nothing resounds through us that we're not a part of, which brings us back to the importance of the integration, tuning and taming practices of Part II. As Kristi reflected on her own journey: "Personal development is the change that changes the system. As we integrate what we've learned, we change the things asking to be changed." We can't just export the learning from one context, such as a dojo, and expect it to work in a hospital. Rather, like an energy translator, we have to feel into what meshes between what we now know and the context we now face. "It takes every day," Kristi concluded. "You can't lose a day of commitment to your own training. That's the real program." But when that's the kind of commitment we live with, we don't show up anywhere without making a difference. Which is how our waves of impact ripple ever further, and the change around us grows ever larger. Next, we look at how change gets really big.

TEAM REFLECTION PRACTICE BASED ON THEORY U—PART 1

As a facilitator of this exercise, you'll read a script of instructions and invitations. Words in italics are the suggested script. Feel for the group's energy as you move through this script, giving each stage time to ripen before you move on.

To start: State a focusing purpose to the exercise in terms of exploring a couple of questions of relevance to the team and each person on it. For example: What is the best and fullest purpose of this team? What is the work and direction of this team? What is my best contribution to this team? The questions could also be around a particular challenge or opportunity. For example: What is ready to happen around this challenge? What is my best and fullest contribution to this opportunity? In the script that follows, references to THE TEAM imply connections to this focusing purpose.

Sensing: Invite people into a circle, initially having them stand in front of where they will sit. It's best if the circle is configured with cushions, but chairs are okay. Each person should have paper and something to write with, at their seats, for use in Part 2.

> *Bring your weight toward your big toes, soften*
> *your knees and let your weight sink into your hara.*
> *Look at the person directly opposite you and, using*
> *your eyes or in some other silent way, acknowledge*
> *that person as your partner in this exercise, and let*
> *them acknowledge you.*

Note: as facilitator, you can identify a single partner, no partner or a partner-pair, depending on the role you want to play and whether the group size is even or odd.

(cont.)

Now, let your view expand to 180-degrees. Drop your gaze to splash off the center of the circle, taking in the entire group all at once and no one in particular. On the next exhale, send the sound of "OH-H-H-H-H-H-H" down to your hara at full strength. On the second exhale—"OH-H-H-H-H-H-H-H-H-H"—let your sound reach out and become everyone's sound as their sound comes through you—no separation. On the third exhale, match the sound to the day, the universe, the whole picture. On the next exhale, keep the same intensity, but half the volume. "Oh-h-h-h-h-h-h-h." On the next exhale, same intensity, half again: "Oh-h-h-h-h-h-h." On the next exhale, no sound, pure vibration. Maintain this bigness and sit comfortably.

Letting Go:

Feel completely joined in the circle while being totally yourself, relaxed and aware. Feel your breath move through your body, easily, slowly, the exhale guided as if by gravity itself. Let your heart area soften and open. Let every sense open to register even the tiniest ripple in the flow of energy, here and now. You can occasionally close your eyes if it helps you focus on other senses, and as you open them again, return to 180-degree vision. Breathe into that flow and let it flow through you, with nothing held back and no one holding—completely supported and completely free in the flow of energy, sensing its movement, its direction—open and curious.

Note: Allow some silence and breathing room. Continue to Part 2 when you feel the group is ready.

TEAM REFLECTION PRACTICE BASED ON THEORY U—PART 2

Letting Come:

What image, feeling, symbol, message or other essence has arisen in relation to THE TEAM? What sensations register in your body in relation to THE TEAM?

Staying one with your breath, one in the flow of energy, when you're ready, jot down any image, sensations, or message you wish to capture, trusting yourself and what has arisen as a true reflection of connected wisdom, ready to emerge.

Action:

What qualities and gifts have you witnessed in relation to THE TEAM? What qualities and gifts have you witnessed in yourself in relation to THE TEAM? What form could they take in the future?

Remember or write down any thoughts or sensations that you want to remember. Remain quietly in the circle with the intention of supporting others while the group is finishing.

When you feel the group is ready: Acknowledge your thanks to the circle and go with your partner to a quiet place to debrief. Listen to what arose for your partner and ask questions that help their experience become more concrete, including something that could be further explored or implemented. Swap roles. Help one another make connections between these insights and the qualities and gifts of the person, the team, and the forms they could take.

(cont.)

After both partners have talked, each person writes or draws a summary of how they could envision the team responding to the focusing questions, and/or their own role in it.

To finish: These summaries can be collected, assembled into a collage, and/or shared verbally. Either way, the group should circle up one more time (i.e., following the *Circle Up* practice in *Inviting Team Resonance*) for each person to offer back to the group: *What stood out for me in that process?* And potentially: *What is ready to come through THE TEAM now? What is my best role in that?*

RESONANCE RECAP—TEAMS

- Merge, flow, or group Samadhi are all terms describing a coherent vibratory state available to a team that represents a phase shift, an evolution of order beyond the individual.
- While team flow cannot be mandated, the four conditions in which it is most likely to arise are: (1) a unifying challenge, (2) interdependence, (3) personal agency, and (4) a way for individual efforts to add up.
- Flow in teams and organizations is more frequently inspired by "flow agents" who are characteristically cooperative, self-transcendent, and self-directed.
- Each of the energy patterns contributes something essential to team flow, and each can be selectively enhanced depending on what's lacking.
- Theory U is an excellent use of resonance to help a group collectively sense universal energy in terms of a future ready to emerge through them.

9

BIG CHANGE

I 'd been teaching leadership programs for nearly twenty years in companies that spanned the globe, slowly introducing the power and benefits of working with mind, body and energy in leadership. But in 2012, not long after the walls were up at the Spring Green Dojo in Wisconsin, where my own Zen training and teaching were taking root, I saw a way to quit working slowly. I founded IZL and started bringing leaders there in self-selected programs that could take them deeper, further, faster than is possible in a corporate environment. And why the hurry? Because we live in a time of big change: from the looming cataclysmic effects of climate change to the irrepressible march of artificial intelligence and its social implications, to our dysfunctional systems and polarized politics. Leaders, meaning all of us making our difference, are in the process of radically re-shaping life on this planet and, with enough awakened wisdom, we might do a better job of it. Building toward this critical mass of more awakened leaders fuels us daily at IZL.

Whether we call it a critical mass or what Malcolm Gladwell popularized as a "tipping point," big change in complex systems is characterized by a phase-shifting moment of resonance when gradual, latent change becomes suddenly evident. We saw an uncreatively destructive example of this in the tipping point winds that shook apart the Tacoma Narrows Bridge. A more creatively destructive example would be the Berlin Wall. It stood, seemingly impenetrable, for decades where any individual who dared to challenge it was shot. Yet when enough social forces added up to a tipping point, the Wall suddenly came tumbling down. In this chapter, we review the conditions that lead to a tipping point and in particular, how we, as resonating agents, can bring about large-scale change with large-scale wisdom. We explore the conditions that are present or absent in some of our current approaches to vexing issues, and climate change in particular. We'll see how the four qualities that spark resonance in teams apply in modified form to large-scale systems and big change. But unlike most models of change that treat it as a phenomenon "out there" in the objective world, we'll see how resonance links our inner and outer conditions, making us truly the change we want to see in the world.

THE MIDNIGHT RIDE OF A RESONATOR

Paul Revere was a special guy. Gladwell uses him as an example of the kind of person who can spark a tipping point, as Revere did in rallying local militia to defend against advancing British troops in what became America's Revolutionary War. His decision to make his midnight ride had started earlier that day with a buzz in the air that a major move by the British was imminent. An unusual number of British troops were seen scurrying around on Boston's Long Wharf and, by afternoon, he'd received a warning from a livery boy who had overheard a British soldier say something about "hell to pay tomorrow." Of Revere's midnight ride, Gladwell writes:

> In every town he passed through along the way. . . he knocked on doors and spread the word, telling local colonial leaders of the oncoming British, and telling them to spread

the word to others. Church bells started ringing. Drums started beating. The news spread like a virus, as those informed by Paul Revere sent out riders of their own, until alarms were going off throughout the entire region. The word was in Lincoln, Massachusetts by 1 am, in Sudbury by 3, in Andover, 40 miles northwest of Boston, by 5 am. . . . When the British finally began their march toward Lexington [the next morning] their foray into the countryside was met—to their utter astonishment—with organized and fierce resistance. In Concord that day, the British were confronted and soundly beaten by the colonial militia.[74]

Revere wasn't the only revolutionary riding through the towns of Massachusetts that night, warning of the oncoming British. William Dawes was making his own ride, but few people along his route seemed to get the message and, had Gladwell not written about him, I wouldn't have known his name. Revere made a penetrating impact that night owing to the strength and breadth of the signal he resonated. The breadth came from the fact that he was exceptionally well-connected. The strength of his signal came from the utmost urgency of his message, his heartfelt commitment to spreading it—this was no half-hearted ride—and because others respected him as someone "in the know." Gladwell teases out these qualities as three types of people who play an important role in catalyzing big change: connectors, mavens and salespeople. Connectors know a lot of people. Mavens are the experts, the voices people trust and turn to for reliable information. Salespeople are the charismatic influencers who can persuade people and move them to action. These qualities may be embodied in different people united by a common challenge, but on that midnight ride, Paul Revere embodied all three.

Like so many tales of history, stories like this tend to emphasize the greatness of an individual, so we may miss a larger truth: even Paul Revere, with all his connections, expertise and persuasive power, would not have manifest his ride without the urgency of the context, and would not have been successful without vibrating with the conditions he sensed. Resonance, as we've seen all along is *relational.* Without the benefit of hindsight, it calls for attunement in the present that gives us insight and even foresight.

THE CONDITIONS FOR BIG CHANGE

So let's take another ride through the story of Paul Revere and see how resonance works through individual, often extraordinary, acts in combination with larger conditions to catalyze big change. We'll start from the four factors contributing to team coherence and see how they scale up to the even wider coherence that is a social tipping point.

Unifying challenge. For big change to happen, there has to be a common perception of the need for change. British colonists had been settling in Boston and the surrounding areas for more than 150 years. The idea of confronting British authority had been treasonous, frightful, and would not have found widespread support in an earlier time. But in 1775, there was a ripeness and reason for change that unified people. How do we sense the ripeness for change? What Revere did was listen, which we know is the input to resonating. Connected to so many people, he kept his ear to the ground and knew resistance to British rule had become widespread. On the day of his ride, he listened to the livery boy and sensed the unrest of wharf activities. He conferred with close friends—another resonance check—did they sense things as he did? By evening, he and his inner circle were convinced that British troops would attack the next day, and he knew people would rise up in resistance if they had warning.

Interdependence/Connection. For large scale social change to hit a tipping point, people have to be connected and feel "we're in this together." You might recall how even the tiniest break in the connectedness of a bell destroyed its resonance. Likewise for social change, people need ways to connect and communicate to make collective action possible. Certainly, to repel a British troop advance, the colonists from every community knew they needed one another. They had already loosely organized into militia led by local leaders on whose doors Paul Revere knew to knock. And being a consummate connector and maven, Revere himself was someone on whom many people had come to depend for accurate information.

The systems of connection and communication in Revere's ride were primitive by our standards. He traveled at the speed of horse, shared his message one vibrating voice to another, got others to repeat it, and amplify it with church bells and drums. His message spread forty miles in five hours. With today's systems, we could reach forty miles in milliseconds, but today's challenge is to discern a signal worth listening to amidst all the noise carried on the channels that interconnect us.

Personal Agency. It's not enough to sense a huge challenge and know we depend on one another to deal with it, we also need a way to act. We need something to do. Paul Revere's personal agency put him on horseback with a hell-bent mission to warn people. But he also gave others things to do: spread the message, ring the bells, take up arms and pull your militia together. In being able to turn emotional imperative into action, people are given a way to resonate with the change at hand. Personal agency also speaks to individual willingness to *be* changed by what we hear. Revere could have heard the livery boy and said, "I'm too busy today," but instead he let the message re-shape his plans for the day. A farmer in Concord could have heard Revere's message and said, "I've got a field to till tomorrow," but instead let the message change him, left his tools in the field, and joined his fellow farmer-militia in handing the British their first defeat.

A Way to Add Up. Just as we saw in imagining soldiers crossing a bridge in lockstep, so too when signals add up they can reach tipping points for big change. When signals don't add up, they become like the choppy waters of Round Bay dissipated against the shoreline.

While personal efforts are the indispensable energy of big change, reaching a tipping point requires a way for those efforts to add up, rather than interfere with or cancel one another. Part of Revere's success was being able to tap into local leaders and militia already in place. Like a spinal column connecting clusters of local neurons, Revere's ride was a way for a lot of local efforts to add up to mile after mile of resistance to the British advance. His ride was a sparking incident in a combustible mixture of unified purpose, connection, and ability to act.

The ride of Paul Revere is taught to every American schoolkid, striking a chord that resonates with pride in the American psyche, including the value of "well-regulated militia" bearing arms that could repulse the British, enshrined sixteen years later in the American Constitution. In its time, armed militia were a way for Revere's warning to add up to the start of a war we celebrate. Transported to modern times and modern weaponry, it has generated a society of more guns than people, with no common enemy to repulse, but only the imagined enemies of our most destabilized and paranoid parts who can pull a trigger and murder a roomful of schoolchildren within seconds. In 2019, the United States suffered, on average, more than one mass murder per day[75]. Tragically ironic that our colonial fight for freedom should reverberate into a social issue crying out for big change in its own right.

And gun violence is not the only social issue crying out for change, just as Revere's ride and the colonial uprising is not the only American story. When the colonists arrived, indigenous people were already in America, and suffered mightily in the ensuing centuries as their lands were stripped away and their local cultures destroyed by the better-armed, disease-spreading Europeans. Europeans bearing arms also started bringing Africans across the ocean and into slavery. Even after the horror of slavery ended, racial inequality became institutionalized in the American way of life—from apartheid practices to access to good education or bank loans to buy a house. In the economic boom following World War II, government loan policies and redlining of neighborhoods channeled the burgeoning wealth of home ownership and better schools almost entirely to white people. In the ensuing decades, the gap in mean net worth between whites and blacks has widened to more than tenfold[76]. In the illusion of separateness between self and other, we have cut off from a part of ourselves and fostered a deep illness in our society. That illness was laid bare again in the spring of 2020 as coronavirus tore across the United States, disproportionately destroying black lives. Then came the horrific death-by-police of George Floyd, sparking viral protests that may yet herald a tipping point toward racial equity and social justice.

This same attitude of dominance and exploitation that fueled freedom and slavery in America, turned toward our planet has created a looming disaster. The planet is heating up and only models that include human activity can account for the amount of warming[77]. Storms are becoming more fierce and frequent, wildfires more out of control, and species are disappearing at a rate not seen since the dinosaur extinction sixty-five million years ago[78].

Of course, our goal was not to wreck the place, but only to provide for our families, advance our businesses, and grow our economies. But at every level, we created an artificial boundary—another illusion of separation—inside of which we asserted our control and outside of which we didn't care. Inside our homes and factory walls, we controlled how we lived and worked. Outside our homes and factory walls, we dumped our garbage. Incessant growth called for incessant energy that we pulled out of the earth, dumping its heat-trapping byproducts into the atmosphere—what we called "externalities"—as if to underscore our delusion of separateness from some "out there" that nevertheless did not go away. Solving climate change may well be the ticking time bomb calling for the biggest change in how we live. This was highlighted again in 2020 as coronavirus interrupted our traveling way of life and, within weeks, cleared the skies over once-smoggy cities. While climate change and coronavirus may not be connected by cause, they are certainly connected by effects. For all the ways we're tried to negotiate climate action by policy, coronavirus made its demands non-negotiable with one result being that we are burning a good deal less carbon.

How does this history guide us in exploring the resonance of big change? First, we're reminded that that energy does not disappear, it just keeps changing form, relayed from one vibrating system to the next. By selecting a beginning and an end, we can craft a meaningful story from some part of this chain, from the ride of Paul Revere to a planet more than $1°C$ warmer than pre-industrial levels, to a virus that challenges our way of life. But energy doesn't end where we choose to stop our story. All that it leads to will include both triumph and tragedy, which leads to the second lesson. Our actions in the present don't come out of nowhere, but rather they're shaped by the energies we vibrate with, and play into a medium where they set off their own chain reactions. As we look at the vexing social issues facing us today, the principles of resonance can give us a framework for recognizing what's present and what's missing in our current efforts at big change.

CLIMATE ACTION: A CASE STUDY IN RESONANCE INTERRUPTED

"Why is this so hard?" Gordon Greene Roshi challenged all of us to reflect on our own behavior with respect to climate change. What's more, why is large-scale will on climate action so hard to amass? While we could take any of the wicked issues I just named and run them through our four principles of resonance, I'm going to focus on climate change because it has worldwide significance, exacerbates all other social issues, and is nearing a tipping point that has been elusive for decades. It was the initial inspiration for this book and is a good case study in how the effects of resonance can be interrupted, slowed down or sped up.

Unifying challenge. The science of climate change has been clear for decades, but it hasn't been treated as a unifying challenge. Quite the opposite: it has been politicized and polarizing, sowing doubt and launching inconsistent efforts that fall far short of the challenge. Climate models and the assumptions they make are complex and, in the 1960s and '70s, there was doubt among the scientific community about the extent and causes of greenhouse warming. Even as the science of warming became more clear in the '80s and human industrialization was shown to be a significant cause, doubts were deliberately fostered by the fossil fuel lobby, and an ever-shrinking minority scientific view was given equal voice to an ever-growing scientific consensus.

Sowing doubt is good way to slow down resonance, because without conviction we don't act clearly. Is it warming or natural variation? Is it us? Can we do anything about it? In 2004, American bestselling author, Michael Crichton, came out with his novel, *State of Fear*, positioning global warming as a government conspiracy. A couple of years later, Al Gore premiered his *Inconvenient Truth*, showing CO_2 levels at unprecedented highs, and calling for action. Maybe if you could treat this as a political conspiracy or partisan issue, you didn't need to be inconvenienced. As linguist George Lakoff reminds us: people choose their frames of understanding first and then select facts to support them[79]. Even as the facts around climate change became indisputable, they didn't resonate with the people who held frames those facts didn't fit.

What's emerging now in the voice and being of sixteen-year-old Greta Thunberg is a new generation that is much more unified around the burning platform that is climate change. They read the Intergovernmental Panel on Climate Change (IPCC) report and are not bound by vested interests and business models to protect; their frame is the future they are inheriting, and it doesn't look pretty. We see resonance in the number of people, young and old, joining climate strikes. We see resonance in the news coverage and social media views of Greta Thunberg speaking to the World Economic Forum in Davos, the R20 in Australia, or the United Nations. Only now after decades do we seem to be reaching critical mass in recognizing a unifying challenge. Contrast this with the relative speed with which we recognized the unifying challenge of coronavirus when our lives, loved ones, and livelihood were at stake.

Interdependence/Connection. If there were ever a worldwide issue calling us to be "all in it together," solving climate change is it, but that is not our current reality. While we may need one another, we can't yet count on one another. Even though we are more connected than at any other time in human history, in the United States certainly, those connections also divide us into echo chambers reflecting the frames we already believe. As Greta Thunberg observed when asked how she finds American attitudes toward climate change different than those in her home country, Sweden: "Here it is being discussed as something you believe in or not believe in. Where I come from, it's a fact."[80]

Again, the contrast with coronavirus is striking and instructive. For a brief time in the United States, the possibility that coronavirus was a hoax floated through various media channels (the same ones that would say climate change is a hoax) and some people chose to believe that. But, unlike climate change unfolding over years, the effects of coronavirus were evident in days: it was killing people and overwhelming healthcare systems. Quickly we could see we *are* in this together because we collectively rely on those systems and the fact is: viruses are contagious.

Having wired up our planet on the Internet and people on social media, the potential for a tipping point around climate change is, on the one hand, greater than ever and on the other hand, easier to interrupt because of all the ways that social media can be manipulated. Joshua Cooper Ramo points to this danger in *The Seventh Sense*, noting how public opinion and even elections can be manipulated: not by manipulating the voting booth, but by manipulating the voter[81]. Social media spewing fear, doubt, and rage, super-amplified by the rate at which bots can repeat the signal, sends us in a race to the bottom of human consciousness where all we think of is ourselves.

Even though our interdependence and connection are facts, if too many people operate out of the illusion of separateness, the bell for climate change can't ring with any strength. And people who do not want it to ring can keep breaking it.

Personal Agency. Al Gore, in sharing his *Inconvenient Truth*, would marvel at the fact that people could go from denying climate change was happening to saying they couldn't do anything about it—without ever stopping in between. What both endpoints have in common is the lack of personal agency which, again, keeps a signal from resonating. Since then, many more voices have joined Al Gore offering actions we can take, starting with informing ourselves— learning more about what really *is* the science, what really *are* the options. Books and websites now give ways to calculate one's carbon footprint and get a feel for what parts of one's lifestyle are the worst carbon-emitting culprits[82]. One can now purchase carbon offsets for airline travel, which is a major contributor to carbon emissions. And campaigns encouraging us to Reduce, Recycle and Reuse[83] have given everyone something to do, even if we're not the ones to invent a better battery or a CO_2-sucking air cleaner.

It's a promising sign that we're moving toward a tipping point on this issue as more people find their personal agency in acting on climate change. Still, the effectiveness of those actions and the belief in their effectiveness are crucial to whether the energy of personal agency keeps spreading and growing, or gets drowned out and dissipated, which leads to the last component.

A Way to Add Up. This has been largely missing in our inconsistent national and international approaches to climate change and has greatly dampened global resonance around meeting the magnitude of the challenge. The whole issue suffers from the collective-action problem, that is: if I inconvenience myself and change my own energy-sucking ways, and others don't, the problem will remain. Yet if I change nothing and expect others do the work for me, I still get the benefits. The collective action problem is reduced in the case of coronavirus because others can't do the work for me; they can't keep me from getting the virus. Whereas in climate change, the collective-action problem is made worse by the fact that the people who contribute the most to the problem are the richest, the people who are most affected by it are the poorest, and the people who will benefit most from solving it are children or haven't been born yet. Translating this into political terms, those with the most clout are most invested in keeping things as they are, those with the least clout will be most damaged by the consequences, and those who would most benefit from cleaning up our act can't vote at all.

Yet political will is an important way for personal agency to add up, creating tent poles around which individual behaviors can self-organize. For example, recycling has hit a tipping point only in places that have had the political will to develop the scaffolding for recycling, where recycling bins are distributed and trucks are dispatched to collect the stuff. Some of the backlash to Greta Thunberg's address to the UN Climate Action Summit where she called for greater political will, was that top-down government policy would not be as effective as bottom-up "grassroots" efforts. Conversely, others make light of the importance of bottom-up efforts if we can't get _____ (name your favorite scapegoat country or company) to curb their ways. Yet top-down vs. bottom-up is false dichotomy: we need the best of both.

The ways we devise to get efforts to add up need to match the magnitude of the unifying challenge to be solved, which again is where top-down guidance is helpful to counter comfortable hopes and myths. One such comfortable myth is that if we each do a little bit, all will be well. Not true, certainly not in the developed West. David MacKay, a UK physicist with a knack for numbers, has calculated what's needed to bring energy consumption into balance with renewable energy supply. "If everyone does a little," he writes, "we'll achieve only a little. We must do a lot. What's required are *big* changes in demand and in supply"—on the scale of ten-fold decreases in demand or increases in renewable energy supply.[84]

How big a change is needed depends on how much hoped-for innovation can deliver to the challenge. But from a resonance point of view, the necessity that drives innovation has to be real; it has to be an energetic signal picked up by innovators and converted into actions, not some tiny signal one can easily ignore and then go about daily business. For example, net-zero carbon emissions by 2050 is an abstract goal; no one feels the pain of that. But when getting on an airplane or going to an office means we could contract coronavirus and give it to our loved ones, we do more than "a little" to quit flying and innovate new ways of working. Would that we could find a less lethal way to continue to bring immediacy to the necessity that drives innovation in climate change.

So, what has made it so hard for climate action to reach a tipping point? It's been slow to build momentum in any of the four components needed for system-wide resonance. We have been dis-united around the challenge—we've been in disconnected, often partisan, camps in our communicating around the issue, we don't always know what to do, and have no confidence that our efforts will add up or be widely replicated. That's now changing as our unified challenge has become more clear, our present has been upended by a viral pandemic, and the future is speaking to us through the voices of our children. If we keep listening to what's true and emerging around climate change and letting it change us, if we keep repeating the signal in our conversations and actions, we will be building toward the tipping point where a movement goes from early adopters to mainstream. In such a super-saturated solution ripe for change, the impossible suddenly becomes possible.

PRACTICES FOR BIG CHANGE AGENTS

I don't pretend to be an expert on climate change, coronavirus, or any of the wicked social issues facing us today. Rather I speak as a Zen teacher and leader of an organization whose mission is to bring Zen off the cushion and to the service of leaders and the better world they can create. These social change issues have grabbed our attention at IZL, as we've felt into the challenging realities of change agents coming through our programs and listened in earnest for where we can be of greatest use. In its assault on the illusion of separateness, Zen, it turns out, has something unique to offer in approaching big change, including practices that resource big change agents with wisdom and resilience.

So how does Zen and Zen leadership approach these social change issues? I'll continue with climate change as the example, but this approach applies equally to other areas of social or business change. Paired with this description are some resonance building practices that can apply to any change that may be your calling (see boxes): *Become the Change* and *Resonance Builders for Big Change*.

I am that. We start from a place of connectedness, which is not just a thought about "being in this together" or connected like boxcars on a train. Rather Zen training gives confers a direct, visceral experience of interpenetrating one-withness: *this permeates me and I permeate this.* "I am that," were allegedly the awakening words spoken by Gautama Buddha as he came out of a deep Samadhi and saw a morning star. I being a star might seem wonderfully mystical, but the broader truth is also: I am the changing climate, I am climate action. I am the rich person who wants to pretend that buying organic products is enough; I am the poor person who is up his nostrils in flood-drenched roadways. I am the sixteen-year old, indignant of the excessive lifestyle of the generation before her. I am 2.9 billion vanishing birds.

Let it Change Me. If I am the problem and the solution, how do I let that change me? Change is not something I orchestrate "out there," but rather something that radiates from my own changed being, from inside out. So, in our workshop exploring how we as Zen and Zen leadership practitioners could become climate change solutions, I realized that I needed to learn a lot more about the state of the climate, where my own lifestyle was most carbon-culpable, and where changes could be most effective. We each committed to calculating our carbon footprints and setting a target for reducing them, using our own experience as data to further answer Gordon's question, "What makes this so difficult?" And then, just like when you buy a certain kind of car and then you start seeing them everywhere, once I had a frame of receptivity for this issue, then everywhere I looked I found information and opportunities to learn, reduce, and rethink my habits. Every day. It was as if I had suddenly tuned into the "climate change" radio station that, while certainly available before, was not one I had been listening to. But once I was letting the information change me, in line with what we know about resonance, it went from being unmatched energy—like a cosmic ray zipping through the room—to energy I could use. The more I resonated with it, the more my nervous system was primed to pay attention to that channel.

Leaders of change have long been advised to "walk the talk" and model in their behaviors the change they're asking others to make, generally as a sign of integrity and sincerity. But the resonance surrounding big change shows us it's even more than that: we won't even pick up necessary information if we're not willing to vibrate with it and let it do its internal work.

Build resilience and wisdom through connectedness. In leaning into wicked problems, it's easy to start seeing wickedness everywhere, and finding others to blame. In tackling inexhaustibly big issues, it's easy to exhaust oneself. The essential antidote is to keep coming back to the experience of wholeness, where I'm not separate from those "others," nor am I a separate "David" tackling a "Goliath" of an issue. This is not a thought experiment but a genuine return to Samadhi. Samadhi is not something we can will as much as invite, using the integrating, tuning and taming practices of Part II, and especially *Zazen*. It is in this state of connectedness that we quit relying on the limited battery power of a separate self and plug into the renewable energy of our whole Self. It is from this state of connectedness that we quit operating with local-self cleverness and tap into whole-Self wisdom.

I'm finding the more I become climate change, the deeper my Zen practice has to become, and the more it's put to the test. Joseph Campbell, the great scholar of modern and ancient mythologies, once quipped that all great religions and wisdom traditions agree on one thing: "Everything is a mess and all is well." If all we can see in working for climate change is that everything is a mess, we will exhaust ourselves. If all we see is that all is well, we don't let the suffering of people and the planet change us. When we can embrace the greater truth that resolves these two sides, we radiate a resilience and wisdom, enter the suffering and give it our best.

Connect with Others. Resonance requires connection, and the more connected we are, the more our signal can resonate with others. Whether or not we consider ourselves to be a maven, connector or salesperson around climate change, if we keep listening and following the trail of where energy flows, we'll find more places where we can connect with others and be of some use. For example, when I was teaching a Zen Leader program in Europe (at the base of a rapidly receding glacier, no less), one of the people in the program used to work at the UN and knew a great deal about climate change. Because I was now tuned to the "climate change" channel, it opened up conversations between us that hadn't happened in earlier programs. She told me of a worldwide movement around Listening to the Earth[85] timed with the start of a UN Climate Action Summit, and how we might get plugged into it. Following up on that conversation, IZL and our Chosei Zen Dojo partnered with others worldwide in pouring our own "good vibes" into the launch of the UN Summit, as well as holding a teaching session in our Madison Dojo and creating a video we could share with our community.

Now, as more people are hearing of my interest in this area, they start engaging me on how they can get involved. I'm still far from being a role model for solving climate change. But week after week, I'm struck by how connection with others on this issue keeps growing inasmuch as I make space for it.

BECOME THE CHANGE

Big change starts inside out. Our own resonance with the change we want to see is the very way we tap into the energy we can work with to bring that change about. In addition to the bigness of meditation-induced Samadhi, we can approach becoming the change through imagination from multiple and expanding perspectives using concentric circles, as in Figure 9-1.

- **To start:** Draw five concentric circles as in Figure 9-1a with your local self ("me") at the center, and your whole Self the outermost ring. Write the big change you want to address in the second outermost circle, along with a particular question you are holding around this change starting with "How might I/we. . ."

- **Inner circle:** Write the names of a few people or groups who you are already connected to around this change and your question.

- **Outer circle:** Write the names of a few people or groups who are also affected by this change, including those who may not want it, and others you may want to connect with.

- **Starting from your local self perspective:** State the question you're holding ("How might I/we . . . ") and starting with the phrase: "Speaking as my local self," answer what are you doing now with respect to this question.

- **Imagine:** Land your pen on a name in your inner or outer circle. Imagine becoming that person or group. Starting with the phrase, "Speaking as {that name}, this matter would be in my interest if ___. My best piece of advice to {local self} is ___." Repeat for several different names, jotting down your answers.

- **Be the Change:** Land your pen in the second outermost circle where you become the change itself. Pose the "How might I/we . . ." question around that change, and answer: "Speaking as

(cont.)

{big change}, this matter is truly in my interest if ___. My best piece of advice to {local self} is ___."

- **Whole Self:** Finally, land in the outermost circle of whole Self— the entire universe holding this change and all change. Pose your question and answer: "Speaking as whole Self, this matter makes the world a better place if ___. My best piece of advice is ___."

Feel into the shift in answers coming from these different perspectives. Feel into what it means to be the big change issue and be even bigger than the issue. Distill your best advice for how these perspectives would change your priorities, practices or actions in the present.

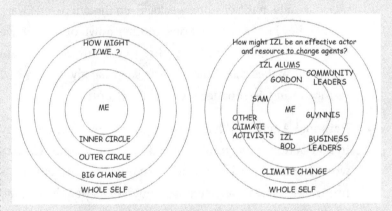

Figure 9-1. Be the change and even bigger than the change

Adapted from G. Whitelaw, The Zen Leader, *pp 233-234.*
Used with permission.

Look to the Four Change Factors for Next Steps. In addition to connection—both our own state of connectedness to the whole picture, and others to us—we can look to the four factors contributing to big resonance for what needs strengthening as a guide to next steps.

- **Unifying Challenge:** What can you do that will give more people a direct experience of the urgency to solve climate change? For example, we found that bringing leaders to a program set amidst stunning scenery at the base of a receding glacier heightened a unified sense of love for the planet and the need to protect it. Direct experience builds conviction. Resonance requires conviction.

- **Interdependence / Connection:** What can you do that will strengthen ties among your community of concern, and keep repeating the signal of urgency? We found, after an exhilarating workshop on climate change complete with follow-up actions, we all went back to very busy lives and it was easy for the signal to fade in the ensuing weeks. Even though people were feeling they had perhaps let one another down or didn't have time for this, getting back together to use ourselves as data for "what makes this difficult" was surprisingly freeing and re-motivating. Resonance requires repetition.

- **Personal Agency:** What can you do that gives others a way to take action? One graphically gifted person in our climate workshop captured our work visually. Another crafted a prototypic Zen experience we could offer people so they could feel connectedness, and a few simple ways to be more efficient in their everyday lives. Several of us built a video around Zen and Climate Change that not only gave us a way to share what we're doing, but offered some actions for viewers. Resonance grows through action.

- **A Way to Add Up:** What can you do that gets action to add up? I don't pretend we have the solution to this one, yet somehow we felt enlarged in our efforts even plugging into the Listen to the Earth movement and being part of activities around the UN Climate Summit. Setting a target and showing signs of progress will also be important. For example, committing to a 30% reduction in our carbon footprints within a year and plotting our collective progress will give us a way to see our efforts adding up. Nucleating activities, targets and progress measures—the sort of tactics you might find in a good fundraising campaign—can become like tent poles around which people can organize their activities. Resonance requires waves of action to add up.

RESONANCE BUILDERS FOR BIG CHANGE

To build resonance for big change, remember that that inner condition and outer actions are both energetic signals that others can and will vibrate with. Best to get them adding up.

Build resilience and wisdom through connectedness. Use the integrating, tuning and taming practices of Part II to increasingly access your own state of connectedness and the wisdom and equanimity that comes with it. If you find yourself getting angry, frustrated, exhausted, or depressed, engage a practice to remember your whole, integrated Self. With the connected state comes acceptance of what is, which doesn't mean we like it, but we take it as it is. This is the crucial starting point for positive action.

What's present and what's missing? Run through the four resonance-building factors to assess where your actions can be most fruitful. What momentum can be built upon? What barrier can be reduced? Any of these can become a "How might I/we . . . " question to which you apply the *Become the Change* exercise.

• **Unifying challenge.** Is a unifying challenge clear to a critical mass of people? If not, how can more people be given a direct experience of the need for change?

(cont.)

- **Interdependence / Connection.** What are your opportunities to connect with people on this issue? Do you have opportunities to foster more genuine connection and less fear? Do people have a way to communicate and support one another on this issue? Feel into whether the connections you're in a position to foster need to be widened or more thickly connected among the network that cares about this change.

- **Personal agency.** Can people act in a way that makes a difference? Do they know what to do? If not, how can more people be shown a productive step forward?

- **A Way to Add Up.** Do people believe their efforts make a difference? Are there visible ways for multiple efforts to add up? If not, look for events, activities, targets and progress measures that organize personal activities and show collective progress.

TAKE AWAY FEAR

Perhaps the greatest gift—and test—of Zen and Zen leadership is that we can be fully activated without being another angry voice in a sea of angry voices. Rather, from a place of connectedness, we can be a conduit for connectedness that others may feel it more, too. Fear grows in isolation, when we feel stuck in a separate self having a problem. Much of what we will be facing into with climate change are fear-based reactions, from people afraid that climate change will wreck their lives to people afraid that acting on climate change will wreck what they enjoy about their lives. As we establish genuine connectedness with people, we literally vibrate with them, interrupting the sense of isolation that fear feeds on. Moreover, if we're vibrating with universal energy and someone starts vibrating with us, they, too, start feeling something bigger, safer, all-embracing. We don't take away fear by rolling up our sleeves, sharpening our problem-solving skills, and announcing we're here to take away fear. No. It is through the simplicity of our being one-with the whole picture and one-with the other that whatever fear can evaporate has a chance to do so.

One of the challenges with climate change is how to awaken people to the sense of urgency without stoking fear and creating villains. I'm conscious of searching for that line even as I write about this topic. The truth is, we do need to break through ignorance—i.e., ignoring of this issue—just as I had to break through my own. At the same time, we don't want to throw people into a state of fear where their coping reactions will make more of a mess of things. What we need is greater awareness, better habits around our own impact on the earth, awakened creativity, and a fearless willingness to enter the suffering that climate change will cause.

I may well die with the fire of climate change still burning out of control, and we have to acknowledge—I have to acknowledge—that the impact of our actions—of my actions—may be felt only a hundred years from now, or may never be enough. And yet, resonating with the Way, there's no other course of action. This may not be our only issue, but because we live at this time, it most assuredly is *our* issue. So, listening to the earth with sensors wide open, let's saddle up and see what we can do.

Whether in service of this macro matter of climate change, or micro matters in your family—from goals and dreams you would realize to problems you would solve—how you resonate is how you make your difference. We turn now to pulling the whole journey together and making it your own.

RESONANCE RECAP—BIG CHANGE

- Big change comes about when resonance builds to a tipping point, fostered by four factors: unifying challenge, interdependence/connection, personal agency, and a way for actions to add up.
- Big change starts not "out there" but "in here" by becoming the change and letting it change us. Listening is when we start resonating.
- Our own state of connectedness greatly affects our resilience. If we're getting exhausted, we're functioning too much like a separate self.
- Our own state of connectedness matters enormously in how people vibrate with us, and whether they pick up fear or a sense of being held in a larger embrace.
- Productive insights and actions around change can come from examining the four tipping point factors point and asking "How might I/we . . . ?" from multiple perspectives and, ultimately, from whole Self.

IO

MAKE YOUR DIFFERENCE

While being an astronaut turned out not to be the difference my life was about, it did resonate with me. It was a job where one had to be both smart and physical—probably the first job where I sensed mind and body had to function as one. And it propelled people into a *wow* state of freedom from gravity itself! While this dream was not realized in the way I expected, neither did it lead me astray. It propelled me into twelve years of studying physics, biophysics, and neuroscience. It motivated me to get healthy and led me into martial arts training and Zen. And it would be in Zen that I would experience the breakthrough freedom I longed for as a child.

The first time it happened was during *sesshin* at Chozen-ji in Hawaii. I was in the thick of another long sit (i.e., meditation period) in a series of long sits, and my body was exhausted. It started shaking. As you know, one of the rules we take seriously in our Zen training is not to move during a meditation period, and earlier I gave some reasons why that's a very efficient way to train. But on this sit, my body was having none of it. The shaking intensified. I worried about being a distraction to the rest of the very still group, and only hoped that my shaking was less apparent on the outside than it felt on the inside. The image came to my mind of being in a capsule, rattling and roaring through a turbulent atmosphere toward space. And then, quite suddenly, there I was—broken free and floating in the expansive stillness of Samadhi-space. Tears flooded into my eyes as I could feel this, *this* freedom, was what I had wanted to go into space *for*.

Even after it became apparent that I was not going to be an astronaut, it would be years before a new sense of purpose would emerge. In those years, I worried a great deal about whether I was on track or off, and whether I could make a living doing something bold and new. I had worked in academia, business and government, from being a research scientist to a senior leader, and none of that felt like the landing point of my most purposeful life. Leaving NASA with exactly two days of work lined up for the rest of my life was the most uncharacteristic risk I'd ever taken. I comforted myself with knowing I had waited tables in college so at least had one skill I could fall back on in a pinch. I also was skilled in Aikido—not the best way to make a living—but it had certainly taught me how to get up after a fall. It gave me bone-deep courage to explore what life had in store for me, after I let go of my plans.

What I see now in hindsight is that, while the path was neither straight nor clear, following the trail of resonance revealed it under my feet. Had I understood resonance earlier, I would have fretted less and listened more. I dedicate this chapter to sparing you such useless worry and inviting you into the depth of listening that vibrates your entire being with the difference that is yours to make. In this chapter, we pull together our exploration of resonance so that you can better sense and make your difference, from how you show up to the tiniest moments, to the large-scale purposes to which you'd apply your life's energy.

MAKING A DIFFERENCE IN HEALING TRAUMA

Alexandra—who goes by Alex—is a research-oriented physician in family medicine who has trained with IZL for a number of years as she engaged in ever-more expansive work with indigenous communities. She worked with the Menominee Nation for many years, running a pediatric clinic treating obesity among indigenous children. "In taking the histories of the children we were treating," she said, "there was a clear connection between the onset of unhealthy eating habits and a point in their lives where trauma occurred." Knowing that food is a sort of "gateway drug" for handling distress, Alex sought to get to the bottom of the social trauma out of which childhood obesity arose. She knew that without getting to the root of the issue, the symptoms would just repeat in one child after another.

What became clear was that the incidence of trauma among indigenous children, which is much higher than in the general population, is a link in a chain of trauma that connects to how indigenous people overall have been traumatized and stripped of their culture. Culture re-vitalization became a focus for the Menominee Community's efforts, as well as Alex's personal efforts, as she relocated to Montana State University to become the director of the Center for American Indian and Rural Health Equity. Alex, a gifted storyteller, became intrigued with the idea of making a movie for kids that would connect them to essential elements of their culture. She had a simple script in mind and presented it to a Blackfeet elder, one of the "grandmothers" who were her internal advisors. No, the elder said, that wouldn't do. The movie was a great idea, but it had to be about the *tipi*. That sounded a lot more complicated to Alex since she didn't know much about the *tipi*, but "Okay," she said, "Tell me about the *tipi*."

"I can't tell you," the grandmother replied, "Because I know it only from a Blackfeet perspective." The story had to be more universal. Alex went to one of her mentors, Bob, who had founded the American

Indian Institute, and asked if he knew the full story of the *tipi*. "No," he said, "The best person who would have helped you was Joe Medicine Crow. He died a few years ago."

That struck Alex as more than a minor complication, but she took it as a leap of faith that Joe would help her if she asked. That night Alex lit some sage and, even if it didn't make sense to her medically trained mind, sincerely asked Joe for help. She went to bed. At 4 am she awoke with a story in her head. Writing it down as quickly as she could, she spilled out the tale of the *tipi* in remarkable detail, more in poetry than prose. She took the story back to Bob the next day. "Yup, that sounds like Joe!" he said. Neither Bob nor the grandmotherly advisors were the least bit surprised by Joe's download. And the movie that Alex made using the *tipi* story has been beloved by children and adults alike[86].

Alex took the work further in concert with the Menominee Community, which was ready to face into its pain and unify around supporting healthier kids. They developed a model of understanding and healing trauma that, rather than blaming individuals, illuminated a path to healing within families and communities. Characteristic of resonant work, Alex points to the effects around her rather than to her own efforts in bringing this about. "It's really the Menominee who have done the major work of using what we were learning. . . to ensure that the entire community is trained in trauma-informed care and in working on cultural revitalization as a major path to healing and wellness." Recipient of a Rockefeller Foundation fellowship, Alex presented her work on Wellness for Kids and Parents at a gathering of fellows in Bellagio, where she was resoundingly encouraged to bring it to an even broader audience. Her work continues to build resonance, and she continues to listen deeply for which of many ways it's ready to grow next. What's been her greatest learning? "Trust the community and trust my gut—not one or the other—but both. Does it resonate out there and in here? If so, OK."

Alex's way of making a difference highlights several success factors, all built around resonance. In her determination to get to the root of childhood obesity, she was tracing the reverberations of the past into the present and finding a point where healing could occur. As she socialized the idea of a movie, she not only got her advisors resonating with it, but let their guidance change her, listening deeply enough to change directions, and even tap into an unconventional energy source for inspiration. Her catalytic efforts were amplified in the work of the broader community to heal trauma. Meditation and physical training gave her a deeper sense of connection and integration, allowing a trustworthy gut check on what she was hearing to guide next steps. And what she's created already with a charming movie and understanding of trauma and healing builds more resonance with everyone who sees it.

These same factors can guide you and me in making our difference: listen for resonance with the past, present and future. Listen for resonance with others and let it change us, making us a link in a chain that leads to more resonance. Combine this with an integrated, tuned and tamed mind-body where we get out of our own way, and the Way of making a difference is manifest through us.

PUTTING IT ALL TOGETHER

So let's put this journey together in terms of a few trustworthy steps to guide you to and through making your world of difference:

- Listen for purpose and let it change you.
- Resource yourself with your toolkit: One Breath, Two Sides, Three Centers, and Four Energy Patterns.
- Tend to both inner and outer work, keeping purpose in mind.

Let's dive a bit further into each of these.

Listen for purpose and let it change you. So long as we live in a human body, the purposes we can put it to can keep evolving, so this is not a one-shot inquiry so much as an ongoing willingness to feel the currents of life and let them guide us. Listen. We know—from a ten-dimensional universe, or from a pineal gland that can sense frequencies beyond visible light, or from ordinary senses that pick up orders of magnitude more data than we weave into consciousness— that we are awash in a sea of universal energy where possibilities expand with our willingness to tune in to them. Listen for what purposes stir.

Being purposeful is an onion of many layers. There can a purpose to this conversation, a purpose to this day, a purpose to this phase of our career or family life, and a purpose to our life overall, perhaps each nested within another, though it doesn't always work out that way. Purpose answers "Why?"—why do this at all? And when our answer is crystal clear, it resounds with an inner alignment that gets us adding up to our strongest self.

Of course, it's easier for us to listen when we're not talking— including the rambling little voice in our head. So, practices that help us listen for purpose are best done when we slow down, in quiet moments of meditation or reflection, and when we can quiet ourselves internally using our breath. One such practice is to "sit with" a question of purpose. We plant a purposeful question in the background—not something to consciously think about during meditation—and sit with the sincere willingness to accept and act on insight that may arise. We sit, senses open, counting our breath as usual, yet this question is working in the background. I often do this practice in my morning meditation, simply feeling into the energy of the day and any purpose ripe for action.

A good reflection practice for doing this comes from Otto Scharmer's Theory U. We used a team application of Theory U in Chapter 8; here we give an individual reflection (see *Listening for Purpose and Letting it Change You*). It invites an expanded consciousness out of which insight and possible actions can arise. We can also step into alternate and expanded states of consciousness in the nested circles of the *Whole Self* exercise (see Chapter 5 or Chapter 9). Starting from how our local self views our sense of purpose or a challenge we face in making a difference, we can feel into a number of perspectives around this topic from our inner and outer circles, ultimately expanding into our whole Self embracing all of it.

The challenge in listening is that we hear more than we can act on. Ideas, connections, possible next steps pop up everywhere, and we can't possibly do them all. That's why the second part of this step is to invite what we hear to change us, and then discern whether energy builds or not. Beware: initial reactions are not always trustworthy. As the hero's journey reminds us, often our first reaction to hearing the call is *rejecting* the call. So, running into our own resistance is not uncommon. Yet if we are sincere and pay attention, we'll notice whether this call or purpose keeps resurfacing in some form. We can give it the "swingset test:" let go for a bit and see what happens. Try something and see if energy builds. If it keeps coming up or energy keeps building, it's resonating with you. Face it, it's yours.

Resource yourself with your toolkit. In making your difference, remember the toolkit you are never without. Use it well and often, especially at moments when you're stuck, or when your usual way of working isn't working, or you're getting exhausted, angry or frustrated.

- **One breath**. Use your breath to settle down or help you be one-with a person or situation in front of you.
- **Two Sides**. See two sides and resolve them to a greater truth when your usual way of thinking is creating conflict or confusion.
- **Three Centers.** When moving in the direction of the difference you want to make, check that you feel supported

by all three centers: the action-power of *hara*, the emotional power of heart, and the thought clarity of head. And if not, return to one of the integration practices to strengthen your signal. If you can't feel inner alignment around the difference you want to make, go back to listening for purpose and see if *hara* or heart have any re-aligning message for the head.

- **Four Energy Patterns.** And finally, when your preferred patterns aren't optimal for the people or situation at hand, shift into another energy pattern and see if that works better. Between the four energy patterns, you have access to the optimal energy for any situation.

LISTENING FOR PURPOSE AND LETTING IT CHANGE YOU

This personal reflection is based on Otto Scharmer's Theory U, adapted to listening for purpose in the form of a vision or intention that is a difference you want to make.

To start: Do a few minutes of the *hara* breathing exercise (Figure 3-2) to shift into a more centered and expansive state. Have a way to write your answers to the set of questions below. Don't overthink the questions; move through each one without hesitation to invite wisdom coming through you, not so much from you.

Letting Go:

1. Where in your life or work are you pushing up against your own edge? What personal doubts or limitations are you dealing with now?

2. Where are your sources of energy and joy? What are the situations when your heart feels most open? What do you love?

(cont.)

3. Looking at yourself from outside, what is your life or work asking you to do? From a helicopter view, where are you in your journey?

4. What are you currently trying to do in this stage of your journey?

5. Imagine you can fast-forward to the very last moment of your life when it is time to pass on. Imagine you can look back and see the whole of your life. What is it, in that moment, you most want to see?

6. Returning to the here and now, imagine that you could tune in to your best future self and ask a key question to which you would get a real answer. What question, if asked and explored more deeply, would be most helpful for you to take the next step? Write down that question.

Presensing:

7. Tune into that question, breathe slowly and deeply, and listen in stillness. Write down whatever emerges from that question, through you. Feelings, images, words, sounds— write down what is coming up, even the slightest signal you feel coming up. Take your time with this step and, when you feel ready, continue.

Letting Come:

8. Write down some of the core elements of the future that you want to create. Be as concrete as possible, and don't worry about it all fitting together. Go with the flow coming through you, and crystallize your vision and intention into concrete words.

(cont.)

LISTENING FOR PURPOSE AND
LETTING IT CHANGE YOU—CONTINUED

9. Look at what you just wrote. Now write: Where in your current work and life do you see the early beginnings, the seeds of the future? Where are you finding the early beginnings—people, places, ideas—that connect with some of the words you just crystallized as your vision and intention going forward? Where are the seeds of your ideal tomorrow in today?

10. If you really wanted to fully bring that vision and intention into reality, what is it that you have to let go of? What old stuff must die?

Acting:

11. What could you do over the next three months to turn your vision and intention into a meaningful prototype, a small experiment, a set of actions? What could you do or create within the next three months that is essential for you and your future journey?

12. Who are a few people who could help you stay connected to your vision and intention, and bring that more fully into reality? These may be people already in your inner circle, or may include someone you're not fully connected with yet, but you have a feeling they could be important. Write down the names of a few people who could be your circle of support.

13. If you truly wanted to bring yourself to what has emerged and bring it more fully into reality—this vision, intention, small experiment, image of the future—what would be the practical next steps you would have to take in the next three days? Who would you contact first? What would you do?

Tend to both inner and outer work, keeping purpose in mind.
When we're on purpose, on fire in making a difference, a risk is
that we may throw ourselves so totally into the outer work that we
burn ourselves out, burn bridges with other people, or inadvertently
sabotage our own efforts. That's why the outer work needs the inner
work, that is, the physical integration—tuning and taming of our
mind-body. That was Kristi's recognition in how she was going to be
most effective in her outer work of changing practices at her hospital:
"Personal development *is* the change that changes the system,"
she said. Our head may tell us we don't have time for it today, or
perhaps we're so tired from a day just lived, we have no energy for
practice—we just want to collapse. Yet there is no fooling resonance,
and resonance is manifest both in our inner state and our outward
effects. If we want to make more of a difference, we have to do more
to hone the instrument that is making that difference.

In the present moment, our resonating instrument is the mind-
body that has been sculpted by the past. But if in some present
moments we tend to integrating, tuning and taming that mind-body,
in future moments, we have a more capable instrument to work with.
As Aristotle observed, "We are what we repeatedly do." Resonance
reminds us that the inverse is also true: we repeatedly do what we
are. In making a difference, something about who we are also has to
shift, and that takes inner work.

A simple formula that I often use as a best practice for making a
shift happen is 1+1+1. So, once we feel into a difference we want to
make and an important next step or a way that needs to change us,
we'd apply this formula using:

One outer practice we could do routinely at work or in our
day. For example, if I needed more of a particular energy pattern to
take a next step, I could make a practice out of one of the "at work"
activities listed in Table 3-2.

One inner practice that integrates, tunes or tames our mind-
body. For example, I could make a practice out of starting my day with

hara breathing and meditation. Or if I had picked a particular energy pattern to develop, I might pick a physical way to cultivate that pattern in my body from one of the supporting activities in Table 3-2.

One token or symbol that keeps our intention top of mind. For example, if I do the Theory U reflection and sense an image from the future I'm trying to create, I might put a picture of that on my desk. The repetition of seeing it again and again will help it build resonance.

Since I do take my own medicine, let me share one way this process is coming together for me right now. This year I have been "sitting with" the question of how IZL can be of greater service in the world, particularly around resourcing those who work for positive change and further addressing climate change and social equity. Listening to this question, I've let it change me by doing more outreach, teaching, conferences, and writing this book, the combined load of which sometimes finds me racing through my day.

I put this matter of being-of-greater-service-without-racing through the same Theory U exercise I just laid out for you. Images arose of dropping into time and expanding everywhere. Being time, not racing against it, I could feel an expanding love and abundance, and see the future I desired already unfolding. A colleague had recently reminded me that I needed to ask not *how* to do something, but *who* could do it. I came out of this exercise realizing I needed to find more "whos"—not exactly a new recognition. I already had a little sign on my desk asking "who?" as a token to remind me to

Figure 10-1. Remembering to connect with "whos" from a state of abundance

use more Collaborator energy. But I could now feel that the only state to operate from in attracting "whos" or partnering with "whos" was this expansive abundance, and that any sense of racing would be my cue to do the inner work of slowing down and dropping into time once again. And there I saw it: a small heart-shaped dish also sitting on my desk—a gift from my sister—with the word "abundance" written on it. I dropped the "who?" sign into it as my new token going forward.

ACCORDING THE WAY

There are many ways to make a difference, but as we've said, only one Way merits a capital "W." The challenge of describing it is that it is not a formula, but instead is a felt sense of resonating with universal energy with nothing missing and nothing extra. Various Taoist and Zen texts point to it in enigmatic terms: "The real Way is not difficult. It only abhors choice and attachment."[87] Or "The Way is level and easy, but people love the byways."[88] Or this guidance from Zen master Nansen, who'd been asked about seeking the Way. "If you try for it, you will become separated from it. . . . The Way is not a matter of knowing or not knowing. Knowing is a delusion; not knowing is confusion. When you really have reached the true Way beyond doubt, you will find it as vast and boundless as outer space. How can it be talked about on the level of right and wrong?"[89]

So, on the one hand, our outer work emerges with the greatest ease, naturalness and resilience when the difference we make accords the Way. On the other hand, the inner work required to expand into this "Way beyond doubt" is extreme. We spoke to this taming process in Chapter 5, by which the ego flips from being a tyrant to a tool. As a tyrant, the ego's choice and attachment is absolute. As a tool, the ego's preferences remain, but if they don't match the situation, we're free to do something else. As a tyrant, the ego loves its drama and identifies as strongly with its troubles as with its gifts. As a tool, the ego is informed by its story, but not limited by it. The more we integrate and tune our mind-body instrument and tame our ego, the more we are changed, both in terms of what energies we're capable of resonating with (i.e., sensing) and the clarity of resonance we're capable of propagating (i.e., through our actions). As Nansen says, we don't accord the Way by seeking it, that is, by our ego attempting to do things it thinks matches the Way. No. We do the inner work that expands and strengthens how we resonate. Then according the Way, like resonance itself, emerges as a physical fact: a naturalness that gives life to all things.

Only you can decide how far you want to take the integrating, tuning and taming practices of this book, but if you find you're not making the difference you want to make, or are getting exhausted, confused and frustrated, try the only solution that I know that works: go further. The more you can resonate with other people, the more easily you can get them resonating with you. The more you can resonate with the bigger picture, the more naturally your actions will resonate within it. The more you can resonate with universal energy, the bigger your energy supply. As you make the profound flip from life focused on itself to a self in service of life, a universe of resources opens up.

But can we trust living life this way? Sometimes people ask me how they can trust the inner work to generate the right kind of resonance, or trust the connected wisdom to guide decisions in their lives. As they train further in Zen and Zen leadership, they often get stronger glimpses of the difference they could make, but sometimes those insights are daunting, disrupting, or even dangerous. They might have to quit their present job to make that difference, or move their family, or work in a dangerous part of the world. They're not sure that they can trust themselves—we've all known times when we've screwed up—or trust life to deliver on what has been glimpsed. The truth is: the difference we can make by cultivating resonance with the Way is incomparably greater than what we can achieve using ego-based control, both in the quality of our life and in the quality of its outcomes. It is also true that according the Way does not immunize us against failure, disappointment or hardship. The two attitudes of mind I find most helpful in this regard are: sincerity and embrace hardship.

By sincerity, I mean engaging life with a relentless commitment to honesty: no kidding ourselves. In that sincerity, as we listen to life and let it change us, no matter where we are in the inner or outer journey, we are Way-making. People sometimes worry that they aren't far enough along for their intuition to function effectively, or for their self-limiting habits to move out of the way. But the Way doesn't wait for some kind of perfection to emerge before it starts functioning through us: the limitless Way is always functioning through limited selves. That's not to say the inner work doesn't matter, and anything goes. But with sincerity, listening, and adjusting, we are continually refining an instrument that can ring its truest note *and* play along with the music of the universe.

To embrace hardship is to extend our energy into difficulties as they arise, rather than cope, blame, or run away. It is to accept that whatever hardship we encounter according the Way is exactly ours to handle, be shaped by, and develop through. Indeed, hardship moments may be when we make our greatest difference. People often catastrophize what might happen if they do thus-and-so; I certainly did this when I contemplated leaving NASA. But it gave me an odd sort of comfort to know that even if it did become a catastrophe, it would be *my* catastrophe—exactly my path to learn from. In hindsight I can see that none of what I feared happened—that was just my ego raising its usual fuss—and the only real catastrophe would have been not listening to my heart, and not trusting my gut.

As you make your difference from the micro-moments of human connection to the grand scale of a life-guiding purpose, it will happen through how you resonate.

- In relationships, get on the same wavelength and your connected communication will make whatever difference is ready to be made.
- In leading toward your goals, listen for resonance and add your energy at the right time to make the difference that matches what's ready to happen.
- On teams, discover the harmonics of working in flow with others, where even you are surprised at what difference can be made.

- In working toward big change, tend to what helps resonance reach a tipping point, and tend to your own connectedness so that you do not exhaust yourself.

Accompany the demands and dynamics of your outer work with enough inner work to bring your mind-body instrument to its most resonant state, whereby you:

- Integrate head, heart and *hara* to resonate your strongest signal.
- Tune yourself to ring your clearest note.
- Tame your ego to listen to life and match its ever-changing conditions.

The result for the world and the people around you is that we reap the full benefit of the mind-body instrument you chose for being the universe. The result for you is the joy and resilience of living your most significant life. As the Universal Energy Concentrator that you are turns ideas into things that matter for the people you love and the purposes you serve, the music of the heavens is brought to earth through you!

ACKNOWLEDGMENTS

This book wasn't my idea, so much as an idea that became me, thanks to the climate action challenge Gordon Greene laid down and Glynnis Rengger picked up. I am deeply grateful to both of them, as I am to Sam Greene, who lit the fuse, and the team that daily sparks ways to bring the bigness of Zen to people making a positive difference: Ken Kushner, Pat Greene, Rebecca Ryan, Cindy Haq, Bob Caron, Scott Kiel, Andy Robins, Cris Nakano, Jen Ayres, Emily Ferguson and Bill Kingsbury.

Resonating—Photo courtesy of Kristi Crymes

The stories of this book give it life, and I offer my deep thanks to those who have breathed those stories to life and allowed me to share them, including those already named along with Alexandra Adams, Dennis Tirman, Bernd Linsenbuehler, Bethany Howlett, and Amiee Bel. Boundless gratitude honors the late Beth Potter for her wonderful stories and lived example of making a difference. Special thanks go to Kristi Crymes for diving in deeply and, together with her colleagues, Gabe Curtis, Audrey Williams, and Katie Davenport, catalyzing wondrous changes in their healthcare system. Thanks also to Kristi as the winner of our Resonate image contest, reminding us of how our impact is forever spreading and shared with those around us.

And, speaking of images, this book would not be the same without the whimsical artistry of Mary Michaud. I so appreciate her deep understanding of what I was trying to convey, even when I couldn't draw it, and I'm grateful for her patient back-and-forth with me until the form and feeling were right.

I offer gratitude to my colleague in flow, Gyongyi Kallai, whose research and generous sharing of it informed my understanding of teams in flow. Thanks also to Cassandra Vieten for sharing the story of Edgar Mitchell, and her efforts to bring science and spirituality into a mutually reinforcing relationship. Toward that same end, I thank Dan Siegel, Joe Dispenza, and Otto Scharmer for informing parts of this book and daily expanding our understanding and realization of human potential.

The conditions under which this book came to life showed the wonders of resonance, which energizes my thanks to Tre Wee and Lee Constantine from Publishizer for their help with a successful pre-order campaign. A big Thank You to the earliest adopters of *Resonate* who pushed that campaign over the top, including most of the folks called out elsewhere plus Ken Meyers, Anita Wolfe, Celeste Mueller, Emily Chiu, Rebecca Krantz, Rosie Abriam, Tim Heinze, Amy Gonzales, Anita Taylor, Cynthia Hartman, Dave Stahlberg, Edith Floeckmueller, Heather Scobie, James Dardouni, Katharine Bourke, Larisa Benson, Mari Lineberry, Nathan Weed, Neil Cavanaugh, Patrick Walker, Robyn McCulloch, Sandra Kamnetz and Sloane Dell'Orto. Without their help I wouldn't have found the ever-helpful and humorous John Koehler, with whom I resonated from the start as being the right publisher.

Deep thanks to Diane Chencharick, Holly Kerby, Gordon Greene, and Noah ten Broek who were early reviewers of the manuscript and particularly rescued the opening chapters. My thanks also to friends and colleagues who have put their support behind this book and join me in bringing wiser, more embodied leadership into the world, including Ken Wilber, Richard Strozzi Heckler, Mandy Blake, Ed Bernard, Wendy Palmer, Kevin Cashman, Stephen Rhinesmith, David Dotlich, David Riordan, Joel Monk, Luann Barndt, Paul Barnard, Cara Bradley, Mo Edjlali, Mark Walsh, and Miles Kessler.

A deep bow of gratitude to the teacher who hammered my understanding of resonance into usable form: Tenshin Tanouye Roshi. His energy, teaching, and writing on *okyo* are behind every word on these pages.

Of course, no project like this works without tremendous support from the home team, and I am grateful beyond words for my husband, Mark Kiefaber, who has encouraged me at every stage of this book, and sometimes had to remind me not to hammer on the keyboard until my arms hurt.

ENDNOTES

CHAPTER 1

[1] You can view a dramatized version of the bridge collapse online: https://www.youtube.com/watch?v=nFzu6CNtqec

[2] It's easy to see waves in fluids like Round Bay or the atmosphere. But waves are equally ubiquitous in solids. We see their patterns, for example, in waves of desert sand, the washboard effect on dirt roads, or in the waves of mountains coming down to the plains.

[3] As an example, see: https://en.wikipedia.org/wiki/Elementary_particle

[4] A force carrier can be thought of as conveying properties that interact with the four known forces, i.e., gravity, electromagnetism, weak and strong nuclear forces.

[5] For more on String Theory, see Greene, B., *The Elegant Universe* (New York, Norton 1999).

[6] https://www.universetoday.com/48619/a-universe-of-10-dimensions/

[7] See J. Dispenza, *Becoming Supernatural* (Carlsbad, CA: Hay House, 2017); D. Chopra, Quantum Healing (New York: Random House, 2008).

[8] R. Ames and D. Hall, *Dao de Jing: a Philosophical Translation* (New York: Ballantine, 2003).

[9] *Ibid.*

[10] The harmony or non-contention of Way-making does not mean we always "go along" or "play nice in the sandbox." Rather it means our actions come, not for our own sake or to our own credit, but simply in service of the whole picture. See also R. Ames and D. Hall, *op. cit.*

[11] *Tao Te Ching*, Chapter 25, Ames and Hall, *op. cit.*

[12] K. Wilber, *A Theory of Everything* (Boston: Shambhala, 2000), K. Wilber, *A Brief History of Everything* (Boston: Shambhala, 1996).

[13] *Ibid.*

CHAPTER 2

[14] I thank Cassandra Vieten for sharing Edgar Mitchell's story at the Institute of Noetic Sciences Conference, July 2019.

[15] I. Prigogine, and I. Stengers, *Order Out of Chaos* (New York: Bantam, 1984).

[16] C. Part, *Molecules of Emotion* (New York: Touchstone, 1997).

[17] G. Hendricks, *The Big Leap* (New York: HarperOne, 2010).

[18] D. L. Childre, H. Martin, and D. Beech, *The HeartMath Solution* (San Francisco: HarperSanFrancisco, 1999).

[19] R. Soussignan, "Duchenne Smile, Emotional Experience, and Autonomic Reactivity: A Test of the Facial Feedback Hypothesis." *Journal of Personality and Social Psychology*, 2002, 2,52–74. A. Attan, G. Whitelaw and E. Ferguson, (2017). "A Practical Model for Embodied Coaching," *Coaching: International Journal of Theory, Research & Practice, 10*(2).

[20] C. Duhigg, *The Power of Habit* (New York: Random House, 2012).

[21] L. Song, G. Schwartz and L. Russek, "Heart-Focused Attention and Heart-Brain Synchronization: Energetic and Physiological Mechanisms," *Alternative Therapies in Health and Medicine*, Vol. 4, No. 5, 1998.

[22] D. L. Childre, et al. *op. cit.*

[23] M. Blake, *Your Body is Your Brain* (Trokay, 2018).

[24] S. Baconnier, S. B. Lang, and R. See, "New Crystal in the Pineal Gland: Characterization and Potential Role in Electromechano-Transduction," URSI General Assembly, Maastricht, Netherlands, August 2002.

[25] N. Kostyuk et al., "Gas Discharge Visualization: An Imaging and Modeling Tool for Medical Biometrics," *International Journal of Biomed Imaging*. 2011.

[26] D. Siegel, *The Neurobiology of We* (Sounds True, 2011).

[27] *Ibid.*

[28] *Ibid.*

[29] *Ibid.*

[30] A. Janov, "Neurosis" originally appeared on http://www.primaltherapy.com/what-is-primal-therapy.php. A. Janov, *Why You Get Sick and How You Get Well: The Healing Power of Feelings* (Newstar Press, 1996, Phoenix Books, 2009).

[31] T. Hunt, "The Hippies Were Right: It's All about Vibrations Man—a New Theory of Consciousness," *Scientific American*, Dec 5, 2018.

[32] J. Dispenza, op. cit., p 53, https://en.wikipedia.org/wiki/Alpha_wave, and http://www.gjcae.org/contact-us/20-music/162-types-of-brainwaves-and-meditative-states

[33] R. Davidson and S. Begley, *The Emotional Life of Your Brain* (New York: Penguin, 2012) p. 214.

[34] T. Hunt, *op. cit.*

[35] G. Whitelaw and B. Wetzig, *Move to Greatness* (Boston: Nicholas Brealey, 2008).

[36] FEBI was developed by G. Whitelaw and M. Kiefaber, and is a registered trademark of the Institute for Zen Leadership. For more on the FEBI or to take the FEBI instrument, see https://febiassesssment.com.

[37] G. Claxton, *Intelligence in the Flesh* (New Haven: Yale University Press, 2015) pp 210-212.

[38] *Ibid.*

[39] J. Dispenza, *op. cit.*

[40] D. Siegel, *op. cit.*

CHAPTER 3

[41] B. Johnson, *Polarity Management* (Amherst, MA: HRD Press, 1992).

[42] G. Whitelaw, *The Zen Leader* (Pompton Plains, NJ: Career Press, 2012).

CHAPTER 4

[43] V. Rueckert, *Outspoken* (New York: HarperCollins, 2019).

44 A. Judith, *Eastern Body Western Mind* (Berkeley, Celestial Arts, 1996).

45 J. Loehr and T. Schwartz, *The Power of Full Engagement* (New York: Simon And Schuster, 2003).

46 A. Judith, *op. cit.*, pp 286-287.

47 Components of this exercise have been drawn from by Tanouye Roshi's lying down Three-Center integration exercise covered in Chapter 3, J. Dispenza's "Blessing of the Energy Centers," in Becoming Supernatural, and A, Judith's sound work with chakras in *Eastern Body, Western Mind.*

48 N. Trivellato's VELO technique in *Vibrational State and Energy Resonance* (International Academy of Consciousness, 2017) is added to the more advanced version on the resonate website. I gratefully acknowledge these sources.

CHAPTER 5

49 J. Bolte Taylor, *My Stroke of Insight* (New York: Penguin, 2008).

50 R. Davidson and S. Begley, *op. cit.*

51 R. Davidson and S. Begley, *op cit.* pp 210-224. D. Siegel, *op cit.*

CHAPTER 7

52 M. Frank, P. Roehrig and B. Pring, *What to do When Machines Do Everything* (Hoboken, NJ: Wiley, 2017), p 39.

53 N. Bostrum, *Superintelligence: Paths, Dangers, Strategies* (Oxford University Press, 2014).

54 E. Ries, *The Lean Startup* (New York: Penguin, 2011), S. Ismail, Exponential Organizations (New York: Diversion Publishing, 2014).

55 J. Klein, "You Can Talk to Plants. Maybe You Should Listen." *New York Times*, June 11, 2019.

56 N. Ulaby, "Crock of Ages" *NPR Morning Edition*, Aug. 6, 2019. https://www.npr.org/2019/08/06/748565582/crock-of-ages-new-exhibit-reveals-ancient-potterys-millennia-long-songs.

57 J. Campbell with B. Moyers, *The Power of Myth* (New York: Anchor, 1991).

58 G. Whitelaw, *The Zen Leader* (Pompton Plains, NJ: Career Press, 2012), Chapter 7.

CHAPTER 8

59 J. Collins, *Good to Great* (New York: HarperCollins, 2001).

60 S. Kotler and J. Wheal, *Stealing Fire* (New York: HarperCollins, 2017) pp 9-18.

61 *Ibid.* see also, J. Dispenza, *op. cit.*

62 M. Csikszentmihalyi, *Flow: The Psychology of Optimal Performance* (Harper Perennial Modern Classics, 2008).

63 O. Scharmer, *Theory U: Leading from the Future as It Emerges* (Berrett-Koehler, 2009).

64 M. Csikszentmihalyi, *op. cit.*

65 J. Katzenbach and D. Smith, *The Wisdom of Teams* (New York: HarperBusiness, 1993).

66 M. Csikszentmihalyi, op. cit., G. Kallai, *Flow at Work*, 9th European Conference on Positive Psychology, June, 2018.

67 *Ibid.*

[68] R. Nierenberg, *Maestro: A Surprising Story about Leading by Listening* (New York: Penguin, 2009).

[69] G. Kallai, *op. cit.*

[70] O. Scharmer, *The Essentials of Theory U* (Berrett-Koehler, 2018), O. Scharmer, *Theory U: Leading from the Future as It Emerges* (Berrett-Koehler, 2009). This work is licensed by the Presencing Institute—Otto Scharmer

[71] *Ibid.*

[72] I thank Paul Barnard for sharing this technique with us. The script presented has been adapted from what he shared, but follows the same rhythm.

[73] See https://www.edx.org/course/ulab-leading-from-the-emerging-future

CHAPTER 9

[74] M. Gladwell, *The Tipping Point* (New York: Little Brown, 2000), p 31.

[75] J. Silverstein, CBS News, https://www.cbsnews.com/news/mass-shootings-2019-more-mass-shootings-than-days-so-far-this-year/, September 1, 2019.

[76] E. Wolf, The decline of African-American and Hispanic wealth since the Great Recession, https://voxeu.org/article/decline-african-american-and-hispanic-wealth-great-recession, December, 2018.

[77] The Climate Issue, *The Economist*, September 21-27, 2019.

[78] *The Extinction Crisis*, Center for Biological Diversity, https://www.biologicaldiversity.org/programs/biodiversity/elements_of_biodiversity/extinction_crisis/.

79 G. Lakoff, *The All New Don't Think of An Elephant* (White River Junction, VT: Chelsea Green Publishing), 2014.

80 The Daily Show with Trevor Noah, September 14, 2019, https://www.youtube.com/watch?v=rhQVustYV24,

81 J. Cooper Ramo, *The Seventh Sense* (New York: Little Brown, 2016).

82 An excellent reference is David MacKay's "Sustainable Energy without the Hot Air," 2009; available at www.withouthotair.com.

83 See, for example: https://www.conserve-energy-future.com/reduce-reuse-recycle.php or https://www.nrdc.org/stories/reduce-reuse-recycle-most-all-reduce.

84 D. MacKay, op. cit.

85 See www.listeningtotheearth.world for more information about this global, virtual movement.

CHAPTER 9

86 You can view Igmu's "Tipi Tale" at https://turtleislandtales.org/

87 K. Sekida transl., *Two Zen Classics* (New York: Weatherhill, 1977), Hekiganroku, Case 2.

88 J. Legge, trans., *The Tao te Ching of Lao Tzu* (New York: Dover, 1962), Chapter 53.

89 K. Sekida op. cit. Mumonkan, Case 19.

CPSIA information can be obtained
at www.ICGtesting.com
Printed in the USA
LVHW010220051020
667927LV00009B/96